A-3

*The Revolutions
in Spanish America*

⌒ ALBERT PRAGO

The Revolutions in Spanish America

THE INDEPENDENCE
MOVEMENTS OF 1808–1825

THE MACMILLAN COMPANY

The Macmillan Company
866 Third Avenue, New York, New York 10022

Collier-Macmillan Canada, Ltd., Toronto, Ontario

Library of Congress catalog card number: 71–89591
First Printing

MAPS BY JOAN EMERSON

To my friends

Preface

SINCE THE END OF WORLD WAR II, INDEPEND-
ence movements, called by many names, have constituted
a mighty force, a major current in the mainstream of world
events. Now an African people, now an Asian nation, now
a Latin American republic commands world attention.
The exigencies of the moment dictate which may be of
temporary paramount interest. Yet no student of world
affairs would deny that the problems of Latin America are,
like those of other huge areas, pervasive and perduring.
President Kennedy considered Latin America to be the
most critical area in the world.

The origins and nature of the wars for independence
in Spanish America—wars that so radically changed the
world about one hundred and fifty years ago—have been
given relatively scant attention in American textbooks at
the secondary school or even college level. Scholarly at-

tention has been considerably greater, but without seeming effect, for so-called world histories and histories of "western civilization" make the barest reference to events that shook the world and whose consequences are of such obvious contemporary concern.

About the English, American, French, and Russian revolutions mountains of books have been published. Of general works on the Spanish-American revolutions of the early nineteenth century, there is only one in English, *The Rise of the Spanish-American Republics*, by William Spence Robertson. That vitally important book was first published in 1918; and, as the subtitle informs us (*As Told in the Lives of Their Liberators*), the author had a very special approach. While much has been written about the individual revolutions, it is well to remember that all of the revolutions were directed against a single imperialist nation, Spain, so that a comprehensive study is very much warranted.

In an effort to fill, at least partially, a very wide gap, I submit this brief synthesis to my fellow Americans and to fellow citizens of the world.

ALBERT PRAGO

New York
1969

CONTENTS

*Maps on pages xii, 2, 74, 112, 138, 158, 168;
illustrations on pages 144–46*

*The Revolutions
in Spanish America*

COLONIAL POSSESSIONS
IN THE WESTERN
HEMISPHERE (1784)

Spanish

United States

British

꩜ **CHAPTER ONE**

Historical Background

IN LARGE MEASURE, THE PROBLEMS—INTERNAL and international—that beset the Spanish-speaking nations of the Western Hemisphere can be traced to the circumstances surrounding their origins.

The news media inform us of riots, revolutions, coups d'état, diseases, hunger, and inflation. Domestic disturbances reflecting the instability of Latin American republics are regularly reported. Citizens of the United States become concerned when the occurrences directly affect inter-American relations, for threats to the internal security of one republic may, and often do, affect the security of the hemisphere. This security and the even more illusive hemispheric solidarity are abiding concerns of the United States government.

Most of the Latin American republics are dictatorships. In those that are not, the degree of actual democracy is

LATIN AMERICA
(1969)

often slight. All suffer from economic backwardness. All have race problems. Where Indians comprise a significant part of the population, there is an Indian "problem." All are afflicted with an agrarian problem. Political and economic stability are extremely rare.

Knowing the historical origins of the Spanish-American nations is of inestimable aid in understanding their present-day problems. Since so many of these problems have their roots in the independence movements of the early nineteenth century, it is necessary for Americans of good will who would like to have "good neighbors" and who would be "good neighbors" to become acquainted with that exciting period of their neighbors' history.

∽

In 1810 Spain's vast holdings in the Western Hemisphere made hers the largest colonial empire in existence (see Map 1). During the next fifteen years the huge empire crumbled; one possession after another was torn from Spain's relatively feeble control by successful independence movements. By 1825 the only Spanish-owned territories in the New World were the islands of Cuba and Puerto Rico.

The loss to England of the thirteen American colonies was trivial compared to the loss to Spain of her overseas colonies. Spain's possessions in the New World spanned two continents. In North America Spanish flags waved over Mexico, which at the time of the revolution comprised what is now the republic of Mexico as well as Texas, California, Arizona, New Mexico, Utah, and part of Colorado. All Central America belonged to Spain. The entire South

American continent, except for Brazil and the three Guianas, was Spanish territory. As a result of the wars for independence, Spain lost more than six and one-half million square miles of colonial possessions.

The sprawling empire included natural resources of every description: the fabulously rich mineral deposits of Mexico, Chile, Colombia, Bolivia, and Peru; limitless forests in much of the area; the boundless, fertile plains of Argentina, Uruguay, and Venezuela; superb harbors on the Atlantic and Pacific coasts, the Gulf of Mexico, and in the Caribbean; verdant valleys such as those in California, Mexico, Argentina, and Chile. The many long and navigable rivers penetrating from the coastal regions to the interior were especially important in the centuries before the automobile and railroad. The inhabitants enjoyed almost every conceivable climate. Magnificent ranges of mountains such as the Andes stretch for some four thousand miles from Tierra del Fuego to the shores of the Caribbean, varying in width from two to four hundred miles, containing peaks among the highest in the hemisphere. There was greatly varied vegetation and an abundance of animal life. And lastly, the most important resource was the people. The colonies contained about seventeen million inhabitants. The bulk of this population —possibly some seven and one-half millions—was composed of Indians.

⤳

The name Indian reflects one of those historical ironies that persist yet fortunately do no harm. Columbus had been sure, and as surely mistaken, that the Caribbean is-

lands he had discovered in 1492 were the outlying possessions of potentates of the Far East, or the Indies, as Europeans called that poorly charted area of the globe. It
seemed perfectly logical, therefore, for the daring explorer
to designate the inhabitants as Indians. The Indians, however, called themselves by the names of their tribes, of
which there were several hundred. They inhabited what
has come to be known as the Americas, from the very tip
of South America to the northernmost points of the North
American continent. The densest areas of Indian population were northern and western South America, Central
America, and Mexico.

There were considerable differences among tribes in
physical traits, languages, and cultural development.
Height, shape of head, color of skin, and facial configura-
tions varied greatly. More than two hundred languages
were spoken. Cultural and social development ranged from
the very low level of the Stone Age Patagonians to the
extraordinarily high levels of civilization found among the
Aztecs, the Maya, the Chibchas, and the Incas. There were
peaceful tribes like the Arawaks and fierce, cannibalistic
societies like the Caribs. Great diversity in traditions,
customs, and institutions was characteristic.

At the close of the colonial period, the Indians were "the
hewers of wood and drawers of water," the principal part
of the labor force. The majority were peons, quasi-slaves,
and wage workers employed in the mines and factories, on
the plantations, ranches, and farms. Only a few had been
fully integrated into the Spanish way of life. Some tribes had
never been fully conquered; they lived on the outposts of
civilization and remained fiercely independent.

Another significant part of the labor force was made up of approximately 800,000 Negroes, most of whom were slaves. The majority were concentrated in the Caribbean islands, northern South America, Central America, and Mexico; relatively few were to be found in Argentina, Uruguay, Chile, Peru, Ecuador, Paraguay, or Bolivia. Together with the Indians, the Negroes occupied the lowest end of the socioeconomic scale.

At the top of the scale were some four million whites. The majority were the so-called *criollos*, or Creoles—those of Spanish stock born in the Western Hemisphere. A small percentage were peninsulars, Spaniards born on the Iberian peninsula; the remainder of the whites were Europeans—a scattering of English, French, Italian, Dutch, Danes, Jews, Irish, Germans. In addition, from the Far East came a few Chinese.

Occupying a social and economic position between the whites and the Indians and Negroes were about five million people of mixed stock. Intermarriage and miscegenation had been common from the earliest days of the conquests in the fifteenth and sixteenth centuries. The principal blends that resulted were the *mestizos*, the offspring of whites and Indians; the *mulatos*, offspring of whites and Negroes; and the *zambos*, descendants of Indians and Negroes. The variety of other blendings bordered on the infinite; the Spaniards at one point listed some twenty *castas*, which may be loosely translated as "castes."

In some regions intermixing of races was so extensive that few individuals of European descent could truthfully assert that they had no Indian or Negro ancestry. Members of the upper classes simply denied any prior mixing. They were concerned, almost to the point of obsession, with the "color question." A definite pattern of discrimination developed. It was, however, replete with inconsistencies. For example, mestizos and mulattoes who were somewhat fair of skin and who were climbing upward on the social scale could legally purchase a document qualifying them as whites. If the petitioner's color was too dark to make such certification credible, then he might receive a doubtful declaration that he could consider himself as white. Finally, however, although color had some influence in determining status, ownership of property and the legal and social privileges granted to large property owners were most decisive.

Whites were obsessed with the concept *pureza de sangre*, purity of blood—a strange concept indelibly related to caste. "Everyone gives so much importance to the rank of caste and draws so much vanity out of it that if inadvertently one of them is treated as belonging to a degree lower than that to which he is entitled, he blushes and holds it as the worst insult." So observed Jorge Juan and Antonio Ulloa, two distinguished travelers sent to the New World by the Spanish king in the middle of the eighteenth century. Those Spaniards who were preoccupied with "purity of blood" conveniently forgot that they were the product of Iberian, Carthaginian, Celt, Roman, Visigoth, Moor, Jew, Arab and Berber—each of which had in its turn resulted from prior fusions.

The abject poverty and extreme misery of most of the Indians and of the Negro slaves in Spanish America cannot be appreciated by twentieth-century man. Dante could dramatically imagine different states of horror in the infernal regions, and a Dante would be needed to describe the very real sufferings of Negro slaves and Indians. Despite the many attempts of the Spanish monarchy and of a few elements of the Church to protect the Indians, their lot barely improved from the time of the conquest to the close of the colonial period.

Enslavement of the Indians had been outlawed, but the colonists found a number of ways to make Indians work under the most oppressive and arduous conditions. Indians were forced to labor for individuals, Church and governmental authorities on public works, in factories, on ranches and plantations, and in the mines under the most barbarous conditions and for wages inadequate to life. For example, Indians working on private estates received a maximum annual salary of eighteen pesos. From that sum, the estate owner deducted a "tribute" of eight pesos. At the end of the year, after having worked about three hundred days for his master, the Indian was in debt to him. Thus he was, in effect, a slave for life. His tragic status was passed on to his children, who were held responsible for his debts.

Debt peonage merely substituted one form of slavery for another. One way that debts would be worked off was by forced labor in the *obrajes,* or factories. The textile factories in Mexico, for example, were virtual prisons, with one portion of the building reserved for shackles and stocks. Punishment was frequent and severe. Work began before dawn and continued until nightfall. Indians who had not completed the required amount of work were lashed and sent to the shackles and stocks. Indians captured in frontier warfare were subjected to forced labor. In those instances where Indians from mountainous or high plateau areas were forced to work in tropical climates to which they were unaccustomed, death quickly relieved them of their sufferings.

Throughout the colonial period Indians were forced to labor on public works. Some of these were tremendous projects like the famous *desagüe*, the huge canal designed to drain the Valley of Mexico. This project was under way for about two hundred years—during the seventeenth and eighteenth centuries. Alexander von Humboldt, scientist, savant, and world traveler, testifies that thousands of Indians, laboring under extremely hazardous conditions for almost no pay, built "one of the most gigantic hydraulic systems ever executed by man." Such forced labor was a principal cause of the extreme misery of the Indians of the Valley of Mexico. Separated from their families, unable to work their own plots of land, exposed to constant danger, decimated by fatal diseases contracted in the intensely humid marsh, the Indians had ample reason to fear and hate the desagüe.

Not until the last half of the eighteenth century was forced labor in the mines prohibited. Nevertheless, the exploitation of "free" labor in the mines was accompanied by cruelty and hardships that continued well beyond the end of the colonial period.

Finding excuses for involuntary servitude of Indians was an easy matter, even for some of the clergy. In South

America friars who needed to enlarge the mission labor force would raid Indian settlements to obtain "savages" who, unlike those already on the missions, had not been proselytized or who had not learned to make the sign of the cross.

Juan and Ulloa also reported that priests often collected high fees from Indians for services rendered. The fee for high mass was four and a half pesos, as was the fee for the sermon, "which consists in merely repeating a few words in praise of the saint." The Indians were expected, if not compelled, to donate hens, pigs, eggs, sheep, and the like to the curate. In many instances when offerings were not regular or adequate, religious privileges were denied the applicant until he had made and fulfilled outrageous pledges. Monks and their mistresses were notorious for extorting tribute in kind and in labor of all sorts.

The whole society was corrupt. It was not uncommon for officials of all ranks to take advantage of the Indians, whose subjugation for over three hundred years had reduced them to a state of apathy. And if this was the unhappy lot of the "free" Indian, what must it have been for the Negro slave?

Negroes were imported into the Spanish colonies early in their history. The laws of the Crown were designed to eliminate the enslavement of the Indians. The compromise that was more or less amicably accepted by the few loyal supporters of the Indians, however, was to permit and even encourage the employment of Negro slaves. Although Spanish legislation aimed at preventing maltreatment of the Negroes, a great discrepancy existed between theory and practice, as with so much other humanitarian legislation emanating from Spain. Even assuming the best of intentions on the part of the monarchy, it was close to impossible to enforce legislation effectively in areas thousands of miles from the seat of empire, weeks and even months distant in terms of communication, spread out over millions of square miles, covering vast expanses deep in the interior regions of the New World. Considered an economic necessity by the colonists, condoned as a necessary evil by Church leaders who found their rationale in alleged Christian ethics, Negro slavery in the New World was a vivid testimony to man's inhumanity to man.

While manumission was permitted by Spanish law, it did not happen frequently, so that not more than 10 per cent of the Negro population had been freed by the close of the colonial period. Those who were free became part of the wage labor force along with free Indians, mestizos, mulattoes, and other racial mixtures.

Slaves and free Negroes provided a variety of skills, learned in the New World or brought with them from Africa. African Negroes were familiar with many aspects of iron work, carpentering, and farming. Of the many new skills they acquired, one is particularly significant—handling horses and cattle. Negroes in cattle-raising areas became cowboys, drovers, and the like.

Unquestionably the spiritual condition of being free improved the situation considerably. No matter how poor the wages and conditions, free labor—especially the semi-skilled and skilled workers—occupied a higher economic and social position. For a few the way was open to becoming small independent property owners. For unskilled laborers, wages and conditions were not much superior, if at all, to those common to forced labor. It must be noted, of course, that working conditions for free men and slaves were about the same as those of similar labor in Europe or in the United States of the same epoch. Spanish imperialism was no more and no less malevolent than any other colonial imperialism.

Between the lowest classes and the middle sector that was developing somewhat rapidly toward the close of the eighteenth century there existed a fairly wide gap. Though members of all races were to be found among the middle class, most were European and Creole. Those engaged in trade and commerce, merchants and storekeepers, artisans, professionals (lawyers, teachers, doctors, notaries), and medium farmers constituted a small minority but played an increasingly important role as the colonial epoch came to a close.

At the very top of the economic ladder were the wealthy —both peninsular and Creole. Of that group, the landed aristocracy—the *hacendados* and the proprietors of the large ranches—dominated the economic life of the people, the great majority of whom lived on the land. The gap between the extremes of poverty, which was so widespread, and the tremendous fortunes of the very few provided an extraordinary contrast. All the upper classes had special privileges, both legal and economic. Those most favored were the peninsulars, especially the clergy, the military, and the Crown-appointed officials.

〜◦

Since Spain's colonial empire was one of the first of the modern era, its political administration was originally experimental and underwent many modifications throughout the first two hundred years. By the time of the independence movements an extremely complex administrative machinery had evolved. Despite cumbersomeness, inefficiency, and corruption, it maintained itself for more than three hundred years and provided the organizational framework by which the mother country could exploit its possessions for the benefit of the monarchy, the aristocratic entourage that surrounded it, and the Spanish merchants.

At the apex of the political pyramid stood the Crown. In theory colonial possessions belonged to the monarch rather than to the nation. The American possessions were administered on behalf of the Crown by the Ministry of the Indies (originally the Council of Indies) and the Intendancy of Marine (originally the House of Trade), two institutions with great economic and political powers. In the Americas the hierarchical organization underwent a series of changes and was headed eventually by four viceroys, appointed by and directly representing the Spanish Crown.

The territories of the four viceroyalties were tremendous areas of land, each one considerably larger than Spain herself. Oldest was the Viceroyalty of New Spain, which consisted of Mexico and its outlying possessions; all of what are now the five Central American republics; Florida and the Louisiana territory (until they were transferred to other powers in the early nineteenth century); Cuba,

Puerto Rico, and other islands of the Caribbean. The Viceroyalty of New Granada, in northern South America, included what are now Venezuela, Colombia, Panama and Ecuador; the Viceroyalty of Peru, what are now Peru and Chile. The fourth, and last to have been created (in 1776), was the Viceroyalty of Rio de la Plata, which comprised present-day Argentina, Bolivia, Paraguay, and Uruguay.

Some areas of special military and economic importance were given the status of captaincy-general while remaining within the over-all jurisdiction of the viceroyalty; at the close of the colonial period there were four—Cuba, Guatemala, Venezuela, and Chile. Within his territory, the captain-general had powers similar to those of the viceroy, from whom he received some specified powers. But because of the distances involved, and the attendant difficulties of communication, the royally appointed governor of the captaincy-general often conducted himself with great independence, ignoring his subordinate relation to the viceroy.

Each viceroyalty was subdivided into political units called intendancies. The intendants, usually Spanish-born subjects appointed by the king, were directly responsible to the viceroy and possessed great administrative, judicial, military, and financial powers. New Spain, for example, was subdivided into twelve intendancies. Since even the territory of the intendancy was so huge, each was further subdivided into *partidos*, governed by *subdelegados* (sub-delegates) responsible to the intendant.

One of the most important institutions of the royal machinery in the New World was the *audiencia*. It served principally as a supreme, and appellate, court for all lower courts in its district. Such districts varied in size. Each of the captaincies-general had an audiencia and ten others were distributed throughout the Americas. In addition to its judicial functions, the audiencia had some measure of political, legislative, and even military powers, all of which were in continual conflict with the powers of the viceroys and intendants. Apparently one of the Crown's purposes was to set up a body that could serve as a check upon the powers of the top executive officials.

That some sort of checking apparatus was deemed necessary is reasonable in view of the tremendous gap in space and time which separated the mother country from its many overseas possessions. In fact, another check functioned from the very beginnings of settlement. All officials, from viceroys on down, might be investigated by a specially appointed agent of the Crown, the *visitador*. Arriving unannounced, he had the power to inspect all financial records and to listen to all complaints from all subjects. Finally, at the end of each royally appointed official's term of office, he was subjected to a detailed and critical review, or *residencia*, conducted under the auspices of a royal delegate.

The judiciary branch of government was in effect an extension of the entire administrative machinery. While the audiencia had both judicial and administrative functions, the former were complicated by the presence of courts with special privileges: ecclesiastical courts, military courts, and the tribunals of the various trade and merchant guilds. Each guarded its special privileges zealously. Intercourt rivalries and jurisdictional disputes were constant sources of friction.

The machinery of local government was even more complex. Of prime importance was the *cabildo*, the principal administrative unit for urban areas and the surrounding territory. Its activities varied depending upon the size of the community and its distance from the site of central authority. The cabildo was particularly important to the Creoles, for it was the one administrative organ in which they constituted a majority. It was not at all a democratic institution, for only the most prominent citizens were appointed to it. In the few instances that members were elected, only citizens of substance could vote. It was through the cabildo, however, that the Creoles could exercise considerable authority at the local level. For major decisions or innovations, the *cabildo abierto*, or open cabildo, was convoked; it included the members of the cabildo plus an additional number of notables. Both institutions, the cabildo and cabildo abierto, were to play primary roles at the beginning of the revolutionary uprisings in the major cities of the colonies.

As in Spain, the city was the hub of political, economic, and social life. In the course of the centuries Spanish-American cities had grown in size and in population. Mexico City, with some 170,000 inhabitants in 1825, was the most populous in the Western Hemisphere, exceeding New York by 30,000. Other large cities of importance included Havana in Cuba; Lima in Peru; Buenos Aires in Argentina; Caracas, Venezuela; Bogotá, Colombia; Santiago, Chile; Quito, Ecuador; Asunción, Paraguay; and

Chuquisaca, Bolivia. Naturally the major ports played a major economic role. Among the most important were Vera Cruz and Acapulco in Mexico; Porto Bello, Santa Marta, and Cartagena in Colombia; La Guaira in Venezuela; Guayaquil in Ecuador; Callao, Peru; Valparaíso and Concepción in Chile; Montevideo, Uruguay; San Juán, Puerto Rico; Havana, Cuba; and Buenos Aires, Argentina.

In the rural areas local government took a number of forms. A subdelegado governed the partido and was chiefly responsible for the welfare of the Indians in the more remote areas. The *hacienda* was a huge, almost self-sufficient estate; it was like a feudal manor, presided over by the powerful hacendado who, in practice and often legally, dominated the Indians on his land. The *cacicazgo* was a holdover from preconquest times when the local Indian chieftains, or *caciques*, held positions of authority in the Aztec and Inca empires. The Spaniards perpetuated the system as an efficient means of ruling over Indians widely dispersed throughout the countryside. The cacique assisted the subdelegado; he joined in aiding or, as was more often the case, exploiting the Indians. The Church institutions of parish, monastery, and mission wielded extraordinary powers over the lives in their charge, especially when they were located far from the principal centers of authority.

The Church's role in the history of Spanish America bears special emphasis, for it was among the most powerful political, social, and economic forces. Catholicism was the official religion of the empire, and the only one tolerated. The vast majority of subjects were loyal if not devoted supporters of the Church. Fanatical devotion was seldom accompanied by profound understanding; for the lower classes, religious pomp, especially the ceremony exhibited on the many holy days, was often no more than a welcome diversion from the humdrum monotony of ordinary existence.

A number of factors accounted for the great authority of the Church. It had representatives in every institution and in every part of Spanish America and was thus guaranteed influence in all governmental and judiciary matters. Through the Holy Office of the Inquisition the Church controlled the political and intellectual activity of the people. Its monopoly of educational institutions, including the universities, further tightened intellectual control. As the official religion, the Church was the arbiter of private and public morals. Finally, its enormous wealth, in particular its land holdings, placed it among the most powerful economic influences in the colonies.

The two types of clergy, regular and secular (all those who are not members of the religious orders are the secular clergy), while duplicating some of each other's religious functions, played different roles in the New World. Many regular orders sent hundreds of clergy, of which the Jesuits, Franciscans, Dominicans, Benedictines, Mercedarians, Augustinians, and Jeronymites were the most important. They served not only as missionaries but as explorers, scholars, and pacifiers of Indians—especially in outlying frontier regions when they were opened for settlement.

The Church was an arm of the secular government under the immediate control of his Catholic Majesty, the King of Spain. This intimate relation between Church and State in the colonies has led many historians to describe the complex as a theocratic state.

The unusual relationship that had existed for several hundred years between the Spanish State and the Church helps to explain the latter's unique position and some of the difficulties that ensued after independence. The Spanish monarchy had the authority to appoint all high ecclesiastical officials, up to and including archbishops, and this royal patronage, or *patronato real*, gave the secular authority tremendous control over ecclesiastical affairs. The Church in itself was a most powerful institution in the Spanish colonies. It was responsible, naturally, for all matters pertaining to religion; it was responsible for the conversion and protection of the Indians; it was the major, often the only, educational institution. It was also the largest owner of land and other property—by the beginning of the nineteenth century, it owned about half of all the arable land; it possessed plantations, farms, sugar mills, urban real estate, warehouses, dockyards, and a variety of other commercial enterprises. As one conservative historian of Mexico, Lucas Alamán, put it, the Church had become too rich for its own good. Laxity, corruption, and immorality had been commonplace for a long time before the outbreak of the wars for independence.

Protecting the faith and the faithful involved the offices of the Inquisition. Little can be said in defense of that institution, whose purported aims were to prevent and eliminate heresy, punish apostates and specified evildoers, and which officially censored all reading matter and all public entertainments. During its operation in the colonies

from 1569 to its abolition in 1813, tens of thousands were
secretly imprisoned and tortured, and thousands were subjected to punishments that varied from mild spiritual
penance to public burning at the stake. Although Jews
were the special targets of its investigations, the entire
community was harassed. The Holy Office was a disruptive
force, creating an atmosphere of fear from which no one
was completely exempt. Secular and ecclesiastical officials
of all ranks were prey to its might. Strife and controversy
engendered by unscrupulous and arrogant clergy helped
to prevent orderly and systematic political administration.

In the eighteenth century, in those countries where
there was effective separation of Church and State—in the
United States, for example—religious institutions were not
obstacles to social and economic progress. In the Latin
American countries, however, even after independence,
there is little question that the Church was a major factor
in retarding the free development of society. In partnership with the hacendados it served to keep the Indians in
peonage and ignorance, hindered agricultural growth,
interfered with liberty of opinion, and gave its blessings
to political oppressors.

⤳

Myths about exotic regions are easily created and more
easily perpetuated. One such misleading myth is that in
over three hundred years of economic exploitation, the
Spaniards did little more than to steal silver and gold from
the Indians and to exploit them mercilessly. The economic
contributions of the Spaniards are often ignored or under-

estimated. Although unquestionably the Spaniards did rob the Indians of their treasure, it is of more far-reaching significance that the most modern mining techniques were introduced to exploit old and new mines and to produce much more than the Indians had extracted in the centuries before the conquests. The development of the mining industry was only one of the major economic contributions of the Spaniards during the long colonial period. Of even greater importance was the expansion of agriculture.

Agricultural development was a synthesis of Indian and Old World cultures. Many products and techniques were borrowed from the Indians. Some of the principal products exported to the Old World were of Indian origin: corn, the potato, tobacco; cacao, from which cocoa or chocolate is derived; indigo, an important source of dye; a number of medicinal plants such as cinchona, from which quinine is derived, coca (cocaine), sarsaparilla, cascara, and ipecac. In addition there were many fruits and vegetables, some of which were unknown to the Old World: yams, certain varieties of nuts, vanilla, tomatoes, manioc (source of tapioca), and a variety of tropical fruits; maguey, the "tree of marvels" which furnished water, an intoxicating beverage, needles, and many other things.

On the other hand, the Spaniards contributed much that was new to the New World. They brought all the citrus fruits and all livestock—for the Indians had no domesticated animals (except in the Andes, where the llama, alpaca, and vicuña were used as beasts of burden and as a source of wool). The Spaniards cultivated sugar, coffee, cotton, rice, and tobacco and created rich vineyards and fruit orchards. Farms produced wheat, barley, and other cereals, vegetables, poultry, and dairy products. Oxen, goats, and swine were raised, and with the introduction of livestock came the development of ranching: cattle, horses, and sheep. Large-scale ranching was a major industry in Spanish colonial America long before the first permanent English settlement of Jamestown in 1607. The *gauchos* of Argentina, the *huasos* of Chile, the *llaneros* of Venezuela and the *vaqueros* of Mexico were all predecessors of the United States cowboy.

Under the mercantile system which Spain had adopted, a cardinal purpose of the colonies was to supply the mother country with riches, principally in the form of precious metals, woods, and sundry agricultural products. Hence increased trade was a natural consequence of the growth of mining and agricultural enterprises. But while Spain received an abundance of riches from her colonies, she was unable to satisfy all the needs of the colonists, especially as their numbers and wealth increased over the centuries.

According to the fallacious mercantile theory, a nation prospered to the degree that it hoarded precious metals. An empire like Spain's which could import precious metals and raw materials from its colonies and export to them manufactured goods and luxuries, was considered to be in an excellent position to achieve political and economic supremacy over its rivals. Spain, however, was not as successful in her mercantilist policies as England. England developed her industry to become, eventually, the "workshop of the world," whereas Spain neglected her internal economy, so that her prosperity was shallow and false. Spain supplied some of her colonies' needs from internal resources, but most of the goods sent to them came from other European nations. They prospered at the same time that Spain's economy declined, especially during the last two hundred years or so of the empire.

Spain became the middleman, to the great satisfaction of her merchants, for trade between her colonies on the one hand and developing nations like England, France, the Netherlands, and the Germanies on the other. Nevertheless, the growth of a merchant class does not necessarily mean the economic growth of a nation. A nation's own productive capacity is basic in achieving growth and power.

The colonists found many ways to circumvent Spain's monopolistic control of trade; they participated in illegal commerce with the merchants of other European nations, whether allies or enemies of Spain. Spain's rivals engaged in many activities to take advantage of the New World's riches. Spanish shipping was attacked on the high seas, ports were raided, and a host of stratagems were employed to carry on illegal trade with the cooperative colonists. The intense desire of the colonists to obtain and exchange merchandise as well as to avoid imperial taxes led to a lively trade in contraband, i.e., banned goods, and illegal commerce even with nations that were at war with Spain. Despite sporadic efforts by the Spanish authorities to prevent it, illegal trade and contraband activities grew throughout the colonial period and attained alarming proportions during the decades preceding the wars for independence.

Between 1565 and 1815, a steady trickle of luxuries from

the Far East entered the New World after unusually long and hazardous journeys. Merchandise from the Orient was assembled in Manila in the Spanish-owned Philippines. From there the Manila galleon plowed through the stormy Pacific to reach the Mexican port of Acapulco. From that bustling port, Oriental spices and silks and jades and many other luxuries were distributed throughout Spanish America or transshipped to Spain herself after having been transported by land across the isthmus.

Intercolonial trade had been limited and severely restricted by Spain in the effort to safeguard her own monopoly and to exercise control over taxes, an important source of royal income. Only certain products could be freely exchanged among the colonies, and they had to proceed through a limited number of specifically designated ports. Reforms introduced in the eighteenth century to ameliorate conditions served only to stimulate a growing appetite; this will be discussed more fully in the next chapter.

Trade with Spanish America was one of the most important in the world. It was so extraordinarily lucrative that for more than three hundred years the great maritime powers of Europe invested a great deal in men and materials to break Spain's monopoly. Wars, piracy, privateering, buccaneering permeate the history of the period. It would be interesting to ascertain to what degree England, France, and the Netherlands grew powerful at Spain's expense.

The Spanish monopoly in manufacture was not at all as pronounced as the monopoly in trade. Since Spain herself was unable to satisfy the needs of her colonies, there were few restraints upon colonial manufacture.*

Compared to the restrictive policies of other mercantilist powers like England, Spain's attitude toward the colonies was surprisingly liberal. Colonial manufacture was growing in the decades prior to the independence movements, as indeed were all features of the colonial economy. Obviously manufacturing was no threat to the economic pre-eminence of agriculture, ranching, or mining. (For that matter, manufacture did not become the principal industry in the United States until some time after the Civil War.) However, manufacture in the Spanish colonies supplied almost all the principal needs of the population.

The consensus of historians is that on the eve of the revolutions, Spanish America was enjoying a relative prosperity. Why, then, were there revolutions?

---

* Manufacture in eighteenth century Spanish America is not to be confused with contemporary machine production. At that time it referred to handmade products—by blacksmiths, carpenters, hatmakers, silversmiths, and so forth—or to laborers working with simple tools and elementary machinery in manufactories like sugar mills, textile factories, and glassworks.

CHAPTER TWO

Causes of the Wars for Independence

IT IS A POPULAR MISCONCEPTION THAT REVO-
lutions are usually started by discontented, oppressed
masses of people. The most heavily oppressed, and, indeed,
the vast majority of Spanish Americans were the Indians,
the Negroes, and the mixed groups—the mestizos, mulattoes,
zambos, plus a bewildering variation of other blendings.
Yet in no case did they initiate the wars for independence.
Some were passive, some supported the royalists, while
others were the mainstay of the patriots. Still others
switched sides. By and large the revolutions in Spanish
America were initiated and led by *criollos*, or Creoles.

Creole was the term universally applied to all those of
Spanish origin born in the New World. The peninsulars
were those born on the Spanish peninsula and now resid-

ing in the New World. Other than that, to imply national or even ethnic uniformity among those of either classification would be completely misleading. The term Spaniard was then not much more than a geographic expression. A Spaniard was a Basque, Aragonese, Andalusian, Gallegan, Extremaduran, Asturian, Castilian, Valencian, or Catalan —to name just the principal divisions of Spain, each of which had its particular customs, traditions, and sectional peculiarities. For two of the divisions even the languages were (and still are) different. Catalan, the language of the region of Catalonia, is a Romance language as different from Spanish as the latter is from Italian; and in the ancient Basque provinces even the origin of the language is still unknown. While Spanish is the language spoken in the rest of Spain, there are as many dialects as there are provinces, along with many variations in customs.

There were many differences among the Creoles of Spanish America, too. They were not only Mexican, Venezuelan, Argentinian, Chilean, Peruvian, and so forth. Within each colony there were notable differences between, let us say, the hacendado of northern Mexico and the manufacturer in the capital; or between the *porteño* (citizen of the port of Buenos Aires) and the independent, semibarbaric gaucho of the Argentine pampas; or between the hard-riding, tough llanero of the Venezuelan plains and the merchant in Caracas.

By the middle of the eighteenth century colonists were beginning to call themselves Americans. The German scientist Alexander von Humboldt observed, "The natives prefer the denomination of *Americans* to that of Creoles.

. . . We frequently hear proudly declared: 'I am not a Spaniard, I am an American!' words which betray the workings of a long resentment." Two centuries in the New World had created a new man. Besides the intermixing of European and Indian and Negro, there were many other influences at work. The natural environment, forbidding and beneficent, the extraordinarily high mountains and the rain forests, the huge rivers, the tropical regions and the highlands, the plains and the valleys, the deserts and the coastal areas—all in their several ways had subtly contributed to changing the Spaniard into that new breed called American. The rough frontier life, the daily contact with Indians and with Negroes—whether free or enslaved— the physical isolation from Europe and its incessant wars: all this and more accounted for the emergence of *americanos* whose outlook on life was substantially different from that of the peasant, hidalgo, cleric, merchant, or lord in a Spain long in the process of decay.

The long-abiding antagonism between Creole and peninsular was noted by Jorge Juan and Antonio de Ulloa. In their *Noticias secretas de America* (Secret News of America—so called because it was meant for the private eyes of the king and his ministers), containing many shrewd observations recorded during their extended trip of 1735– 46, they remarked:

To be a European is cause enough for hostility to the Creoles, and to have been born in the Indies is sufficient reason for hating Europeans. This ill-will reaches such a pitch that in some ways it surpasses the rabid hatred which two countries in open war feel for one another, since while with these there is usually a limit to vituperation and insult, with the Spaniards of Peru you will find none. And far from this discord being alleviated by closer contact between the two parties, by family ties, and by other means which might be thought likely to promote unity and friendship, what happens is the reverse— discord grows constantly worse, and the greater the contact between Spaniard and Creole the fiercer the fires of dissension; rancor is constantly renewed, and *the fire becomes a blaze that cannot be put out.*

Juan and Ulloa's prophetic vision of the 1740's became the reality of the 1810's.

The Creoles had practical grounds for dissent. From the very beginning the Spanish monarchs maintained a policy of appointing Spaniards dispatched from the motherland to the highest administrative, religious, and military posts in the colonies. Such king's representatives, months distant in communication, equipped of necessity with great executive powers, and confronting strong-willed men, had to have absolute loyalty to the monarch. It seemed logical and wise that such men should be temporary appointees who would normally return to Spain to be replaced by loyal Spaniards personally known to the king or his close advisers. Permanent residents in the New World could conceivably prove to be much too independent and more difficult to subject to the absent king's will. It was also natural that the resentment of the Creoles to such favoritism increased throughout the three centuries of Spanish colonial imperialism. Opposition to such favoritism was an abiding complaint of the English colonists in North America, and it has been typical of colonists in more recent times. As some Creoles became wealthier, and increasingly proud of a long heritage in the New World, the demand for reforms accelerated. Sons of these Creoles, often educated abroad, found that the careers open to their talents were limited by the restrictive policy of the Spanish monarchs.

The plaint of the Creoles did not go completely unheeded. From time to time some reforms were granted. The Hapsburgs (the last of the Spanish branch of the family died in 1700) opened some American posts to Creoles, except for the highest offices like those of viceroy, president of an audiencia, or top military commander. Such offices as were made available carried a price that the wealthier Creoles were often in a better position to pay than their Spanish competitors. Besides partially satisfying the demands of the colonists, the monarchy gained additional revenue. Reforms continued under the enlightened aegis of the Bourbons, the first of whom ascended the throne in 1700. During the reign of Charles III (1759–88) undoubtedly the most enlightened monarch ever to rule Spain, a larger number of Creoles were nominated as junior officers in the colonial militia. Creoles were also appointed as subdelegados and received other relatively high administrative posts. Finally—exercising the rights accruing to the patronato real—Charles appointed Creoles to many religious offices previously denied them.

Most Creoles were not extremely wealthy or even moderately so. For such, the attainment of bureaucratic positions entailed more than status. Although most officials' salaries were not high, the financial rewards that gravitate toward officeholders were easily obtained; graft and corruption in general are as old as bureaucracies. After a short stay in the colonies, many Spanish office-holders returned to Spain with riches great enough to provide for an early and luxurious retirement. Though the sons of wealthy Creoles did not desire such posts primarily for monetary rewards, less fortunate Creoles envied these Europeans who had no lasting roots in the colonies. Thus, all sectors of the Creole group—from the poor to the very rich—had sufficient reason to envy the peninsulars. Nevertheless, so far as the reforms went, they seemed merely to create an appetite for more. By the beginning of the nineteenth century Creoles held a majority of bureaucratic positions, but generally they were not permitted to occupy the topmost offices.

Creoles visiting Spain were treated disdainfully and sometimes with suspicion by royalty and the aristocracy. Consider the strange occurrence in March of 1804, when all foreigners in the Spanish capital were peremptorily ordered to leave (because, said the incompetent government of Charles IV, there was not enough bread!). To Charles's peculiar way of thinking, "foreigners" included all Creoles! One of the Creoles thus insulted was the future liberator, the young Simón Bolívar, son of a distinguished and wealthy plantation owner of Venezuela.

A Chilean historian has summarized the symptoms of hostility between Creoles and peninsulars: the Spaniard thought of the Creole as inferior, frivolous, lazy, superficial, "a bastard offshoot of his race"; while the Creole regarded the Spaniards (whom he derogatorily called *chapetones* or *gachupines*) as stupid, clumsy horsemen, unable to adapt to frontier life in particular or to colonial life in general, miserly, avaricious, and as upstarts who sought "a monopoly of wealth, jobs, and the richest heiresses."

Causes for resentment, alienation, and frustration were expressed by Bolívar in an impassioned letter written in Jamaica September 6, 1815, to an unidentified Englishman:

Americans under the existing Spanish system occupy a position in society no better than that of serfs suitable for labor, or at best that of mere consumers; and perhaps the situation is worse today than ever before. And even this status is surrounded with galling restrictions, such as the prohibition against the cultivation of European crops, the existence of royal monopolies, or the ban on factories of a kind that the Peninsula does not possess. To this add the exclusive trading privileges, even in articles of prime necessity, and the barriers between American provinces, designed to prevent mutual trade, traffic, and understanding. In short, do you wish to know what our future was?—simply the cultivation of the fields of indigo, grain, coffee, sugar cane, cacao, and cotton; raising cattle on the empty plains; hunting wild game in the wilderness; digging in the earth to mine gold for the insatiable rapacity of Spain.

Much of what he charged was undoubtedly exaggerated; much was true. Indians and Negroes were virtually serfs and worse, but not the Creoles. The economic situation was not quite so bleak as he described, for at the time of the outbreak of the wars for independence the colonies were enjoying relative prosperity. What *was* true was the very real resentment that the Creoles felt toward the many restrictions and trade limitations. The revolutions were to take place not at a time when the colonial economies were on the wane but when the Creoles—and some others—believed that they could do much better without the heavy presence of imperialist Spain.

ᗡᘻ

In the eighteenth century the new dynasty of Spanish rulers, the Bourbons, made serious attempts to resolve the problems of their discontented American subjects.

From Philip V, the first Spanish Bourbon (1700–46), through the successive reigns of Ferdinand VI (1746–59), the energetic Charles III (1759–88), and the indolent, fatuous Charles IV (1788–1808), a series of political and economic reforms helped unwittingly to develop the preconditions for revolt in the colonies.

It is not at all coincidental that many of the reforms were introduced during the first stages of the Industrial Revolution. Beginning in England, the Industrial Revolution developed unevenly on the Continent and continued uninterrupted into the twentieth century. The growth of the factory system, the rise of the industrial bourgeoisie and working classes, the development of theoretical and applied science, the growth of urban areas and the attendant problems—these consequences of the Industrial Revolution have transformed world history and affected all men and nations.

It is in the eighteenth century also that the Enlighten-

ment—that great intellectual movement which popularized
the ideas of freedom, reason, humanitarianism, and revolutionary changes in the physical sciences—had such influence
upon the so-called "enlightened despots" in whose reigns
so many reforms were initiated. Social change throughout
the Spanish empire was being affected simultaneously by
internal as well as external forces, by man-made changes
as well as by profound transformations in the internal
structure of society, by changes occurring at the centers of
development and moving to the periphery, all interacting
in unforeseen and unforeseeable ways, with unpredictable
consequences. A complex web of industrialism, capitalism,
democracy; of revolution in philosophy and the sciences;
of nationalism and colonialism; of political, social and economic revolution, was in process of encircling the globe,
and is operative still.

The Bourbon reforms were largely the consequence of
these broad changes and themselves were part of the forces
then changing the world. How they contributed to the
independence movements in the Americas requires careful analysis.

One cause of reform was the desperate need for increased
revenue, owing to the expenses incurred in the interminable wars of the eighteenth century. The installation of the
first Bourbon king, Philip V, occasioned the War of Spanish Succession, 1701–17. There followed war with France
(1718–20); with France and England (1727–29); against
Austria (1733–38); and the War of Jenkins' Ear (1739–41),
which merged into the War of the Austrian Succession
(1740–48). In 1762 Spain was embroiled in the Seven Years'

War, in the course of which she temporarily lost Cuba and the Philippines. Those possessions were returned by the Treaty of Paris, but Spain had to cede Florida to England, while France, as compensation for her ally, ceded western Louisiana to Spain. In 1779, Spain joined France in the War of American Independence, and regained Florida. From 1793 to 1795, Spain was England's ally in war against France, only to find herself France's ally in war against England in 1796–1800. For six months in 1801 Spain was at war with Portugal; in 1805, Spain joined France in the War of the Third Coalition. In 1807 Napoleon invaded the peninsula, and Spain suffered from war and internal rebellion until his ultimate defeat in 1814.

During those more than one hundred years of conflict, it was expected that the colonies would prove to be an unending source of riches and income. Colonial resentment against the burdens of taxation was natural. It is surprising, however, that there is little evidence of resentment against the bewildering twists and turns of policy which found Spain now on England's side, now with France. The colonists did not question the wisdom of Spain's military adventures but they resented having to pay for them.

To increase revenue, the Crown eliminated the feudal system of tax farming and substituted a more efficient and rigorous system of royal collectors. The former institution involved the employment of private individuals who collected taxes on a kind of commission basis. The method was not only inefficient but also invariably corrupt. The royal collectors proved more efficient, collecting more revenue for the Crown even though some tax rates were reduced.

Some of the other economic reforms, likewise calculated to augment Spain's wealth, managed also to stimulate the already growing prosperity of the colonies. For example, the improvement of the intercolonial postal system had a salutary effect upon commerce. Encouraging commerce was a primary aim of the reformers, notwithstanding any ulterior motives. Charles III enlisted the intelligent aid of such counselors as the Count of Aranda, a friend of Voltaire, and of other distinguished personalities of the Enlightenment—the Count of Floridablanca, the Count of Campomanes, and the Marquis Jovellanos. All were extraordinarily capable men who hoped to eliminate abuses and stimulate the economic and intellectual growth of the Spanish empire.

Reforms were instituted to reduce trade restrictions and thereby meet the colonists' determination to profit from a Europe undergoing rapid economic development. Previously, all traffic between Spain and her colonies had to go through the ports of Cádiz and Seville; under the reforms Alicante, Cartagena, Málaga, Barcelona, Santander, Coruña, and Gijón were established as ports of entry and departure. Whereas in the past all trade from the colonies had to pass through one or two Caribbean ports, under the reforms many major ports of the American empire could trade directly with Spain. In the past, intercolonial trade was severely limited, and although the royal laws were often flouted, their existence restricted what could have been an extremely lucrative as well as useful commerce. Though all prohibitions were not removed and not all provinces were directly or equally affected, the new decrees liberalized intercolonial trade to the point that the Americas were much nearer to genuine economic freedom.

One purpose of the reforms was to eliminate or at least severely curtail a flourishing illegal trade. Obviously such trade meant a loss of revenue to the Crown and cut into the monopolistic privileges of Spanish merchants. Another important reason for stopping such trade was that from time to time the colonists carried on commerce with Spain's enemies. The profit motive was often far greater than any sense of patriotism toward Spain; and because of the continual warfare and change of allies, it was relatively easy for the colonists to trade with some enemy or other of the mother country. In addition, trade of certain commodities among the provinces was expressly forbidden by Spanish laws. But such laws were either unenforceable or were widely disregarded. As in the case of so many other laws—and they were abundant—distance enabled the colonists to follow their own desires. A common saying in the colonies was *"Obedezco, pero no cumplo"*—"I obey, but I do not comply." This expressed a superficial loyalty to the Crown that did not necessarily include carrying out either the spirit or the letter of the law. Citizens and officials who were anywhere from three weeks to four months distant from the viceroy or from Seville were able easily to argue against obeying a law that they found distasteful. The king, or viceroy, simply did not know precisely what local conditions were, said the noncomplying citizen, or he never would have permitted a certain law's adoption. In any case, the authorities in Spain had no effective way of ascertaining whether laws were being enforced until long after damage may have been done.

It is exceedingly difficult to measure the success of the Spanish economic reforms; while revenue was increased, illegal trade continued to flourish and probably increased, for the Spanish fleet and other law enforcement agencies were unable to cover such a wide expanse of territory. The wily and understandably greedy colonists took advantage of every opportunity, and there were many—so that smuggling and illegal trade in all forms flowered.

Spain's need to build up its navy and merchant fleet led to the adoption of laws encouraging Spanish import of colonial woods. The tariff structure in general was reorganized to encourage the importation of many American products. Both tariffs and some custom duties were lowered. An old tax known as the *alcabala*, a sort of sales tax on all goods in transfer, was reduced; custom duties on goods imported into the colonies were also reduced.

Far from neglecting her colonies, Bourbon Spain did much to strengthen ties. In addition to direct economic reforms, a broad series of educational measures aimed at general economic improvement were promoted throughout the reign of Charles III, and, having picked up some natural momentum, continued through much of the rule of Charles IV.

Of paramount interest to the mother country was the success of the many mining enterprises in the colonies. The Crown encouraged the scientific study of minerals, exploiting scientific talent in Europe. Spanish scientists were sent to European countries to study the latest developments and foreign mining experts were sent to the Americas. In 1788 Baron von Nordenflicht went to South America charged with directing and advising Peruvian and Bolivian mine operators. At the same time Fausto de Elhuyar left Spain to become director-general of the mines in Mexico, while his brother, Juan José, became supervisor of mines in New Granada. Each headed a group of trained metallurgists and mining experts. In New Spain (Mexico), the old and quite natural interest of the local owners had led to the formation of a School of Mines which, under Elhuyar's superlative direction, developed into a most important intellectual and research center. Humboldt considered it one of the outstanding mining schools in the Western Hemisphere, including the science schools in the United States.

One effect of such paternal encouragement was the opening of more silver and gold mines. This, together with improvements in techniques, brought about an increase in production, particularly in Chile, Bolivia, Peru, and New Spain. The latter viceroyalty, during the last decades of the colonial period, accounted for about 60 per cent of the total value of silver and gold mined in Spanish America. How significant that total value was is readily seen when compared with world production about 1800; Spanish American production was close to 90 per cent of the world total! It is no wonder, therefore, that Spain had exceedingly jealous rivals during the entire colonial period.

Successful mining operations inevitably stimulated other

branches of the economy. The value of agricultural production, which remained the foremost industry, was in turn accelerated by the growth of mining. The mining towns had to be supplied with food; with mules, horses, and donkeys; with a variety of leather goods; with tallow (used in the manufacture of soap and, more important for mining, in the manufacture of candles); with cotton clothing, and so on. All related industries, especially textiles and manufacturing, as well as commerce itself, were greatly benefited by the growth of so major a productive enterprise as mining. Each major discovery attracted settlers from all over the empire. The rushes which had characterized so many of the earlier settlements were continually repeated. The dream of untold riches, repeatedly realized by a few, was constantly being held out to prospectors, plantation owners, ranchers, manufacturers, and merchants. Gold and silver lured adventurers, prostitutes, foreigners, bandits, the already rich as well as the needy.

The economic reforms of the Bourbons, whether viewed as measures that merely stimulated a lusty economy or helped bring about an expanding economy, are considered nevertheless among the causes of the wars for independence. It was not a dying economy, which conceivably might have aroused deep resentment, but a relatively prosperous one that spurred those Creoles who became revolutionists. In any case, the reforms were too little and they came too late. To the degree that there was an elimination of abuses and improvement in the general well-being of the colonists, the reforms served to stimulate a hunger for more. The partial elimination of restrictive monopoly practices and the opening of more ports led to the desire for genuine freedom of trade. Colonial merchants of Creole stock resented the remaining monopoly privileges of the Spanish merchants. Removing some restrictions on inter-colonial commerce led to the demand for the elimination of all. Each reform became a wedge; the gaps opened up vistas of greater opportunities for those who felt shackled, no matter how lightly.

Intimately related to the economic reforms of the eighteenth century were political innovations. The creation of intendancies, in full operation by 1790, had three principal aims: to centralize colonial administration more effectively so that the Crown would have more control over office-holders who previously had been subordinate only to vice-regal and audiencia authority; to eliminate notoriously corrupt and inefficient officeholders; and finally, to increase royal revenue by controlling its sources more tightly. The intendants who were royally appointed during the Bourbon period proved to be, for the most part, superior to earlier supervisors, yet it is questionable whether their efficiency endeared them to the colonists, who had been used to taking advantage of the lax administrations of the past.

The subdelegados who were to administer the partidos, or subdivisions of the intendancy, replaced the *corregidores*, the officials whose functions brought them into contact with the Indians in the hinterland. Corregidores had continually been accused of maltreating their charges, in flagrant violation of the laws of the Indies. From the sixteenth century on the policy of the Spanish monarchs had been manifestly humane and paternalistic, in a vain effort to Christianize and Europeanize the millions of Indians who automatically had become their subjects. An unending stream of laws, including the prohibition of the enslavement of Indians, demonstrated the real concern of the Spanish kings to protect and to aid the "heathen." With some noteworthy exceptions, however, the laws were generally violated or ignored throughout the long colonial history.

Among the several ways of exploiting the defenseless Indians was the distorted application by the corregidor of the *repartimiento,* the right to distribute all sorts of goods throughout his territory. The Indians were compelled to buy not only necessities but also luxuries and useless items. Beardless Indians might have to purchase razors, or shoeless Indians living in the most primitive conditions might be made to purchase silk stockings. The crime was compounded in that the Indians bought on time and at outrageously high prices determined by the corregidor. Not too unwilling partners to the robbery were the caciques, or local Indian chiefs, who stood to profit from some of the leavings. The cacique had the responsibility of collecting the debts and forwarding payments to the corregidor. Failure to pay led to debt peonage, the oppressive system of forced labor that often amounted to slavery.

The repartimiento was only one of many abuses which made a farce of official Indian policy. Therefore, one of the principal purposes of replacing the corregidor system with that of the subdelegates was the elimination of long-standing inequities and the effective execution of the

Crown's Indian policies. But the malpractices of the past continued almost unabated, for many of the former corregidors were appointed as subdelegates. Apparently men of good will and administrative ability were hard to find. Further, the huge distances that separated the subdelegate from more responsible authority enabled him, as it had his predecessor, to write his own laws or to interpret existing laws as he saw fit. *"Obedezco pero no cumplo"* could and did cover a multitude of sins.

The political reforms, like the economic reforms they accompanied, proved to be inadequate and tardy. At best they seem to have pointed up the legitimacy of the centuries of complaints. Inevitably more colonists attained a clearer perception of their situation, especially as the way was made brighter by the torches of the Enlightenment.

~⤝

The great intellectual movement known as the Enlightenment swept through western Europe and was powerful enough to reach the Americas, there to have a concrete, although unmeasurable, effect. Originating in the seventeenth century with great scientists such as Newton in England, Leibnitz in Germany, and Descartes in France, this great current of thought affected men of letters, philosophers, educators, political theorists, economists, statesmen, scientists, and artists. The theory of gravitation, the invention of calculus, the tremendous strides in physics and chemistry led men to pin their faith on reason.

The roll call of the great intellects of the eighteenth century is impressive in number and in weight of influ-

ence, an influence that has continued far beyond their
lifetimes. Consider the political writings of Jefferson,
Montesquieu, Paine; include the brilliant philosophers
Voltaire, Diderot, d'Holbach, Raynal, Helvétius, Condillac,
Condorcet, Rousseau, Hume; add the natural scientists
Buffon, Franklin, Laplace, Lavoisier, Linnaeus, Lamarck;
the political economists Smith, Petty, Quesnay, Turgot,
and the scores of men of letters and artists—it is difficult
to match such an array of genius in any century of modern
times.

The ideas of the Enlightenment that capture the minds
of men of good will today are the abstract ideals of humanitarianism and the perfectibility of man; and an emphasis
on science and its elusive partner, reason. The philosophers
assailed the fortresses of revealed religion. They rejected
faith and classical authority and replaced them with the
god of reason and an insistence on experimental investiga-
tion. Of prime significance was the constant effort of men
of the eighteenth century to promote useful knowledge—
such as commerce, agriculture, the industrial arts, the
science of government, and even history.

Of all this complex of ideas that characterized the age,
the promotion of useful knowledge had the greatest impact
in Spain and her colonies, especially in its practical application. For the antireligious works of a Voltaire and the politically revolutionary works of a Locke or a Paine were
scarcely acceptable fare in conservative Catholic Spain—at
home or in her possessions. What captured the imagination
of the Bourbon monarchs, their enlightened ministers,
some men of industry and commerce, and men of letters—

both metropolitan and colonial—was the promotion of utilitarian knowledge. This particular aspect of the Enlightenment could be welcomed by conservative and liberal alike; the conservative could favor reforms in the hope of maintaining the political and social *status quo,* while the progressive mind could envisage more far-reaching consequences.

Ideas, even forbidden ones, have strange but often simple ways of crossing political and other such artificial boundaries and of passing unheeded through customs barriers. The ideas of the Enlightenment came to the New World in several ways. The sons of wealthy Creoles who traveled in Europe came in direct contact with the brilliant intellects of the time. Men of science, as has already been noted, were sent to the Americas. Foreign ships brought not only cargoes of merchandise, but travelers and crews; captains and ordinary seamen all had ample opportunity to talk with colonists eager to discuss whatever was new and exotic, from the most mundane matters to highly esoteric and even revolutionary discourse.

Books of the great figures of the Enlightenment found their way into the Americas in two ways. Those that were not expressly forbidden by the Holy Office made the trip as ordinary merchandise. Those forbidden entered the colonies and passed from one province to another as contraband. Centuries of experience enabled smugglers to overcome legal obstacles. Books were concealed in wine casks and other unlikely places; officials were bribed; prohibited works were ordered by some of the clergy on the pretense that it was necessary for them to familiarize them-

selves with the precise nature of the alleged heresy in order
to ferret it out; books with innocent titles in fact contained
ideas that were novel if not inflammatory. In a word, all the
ingenuity imaginable was employed to obtain books eagerly
sought by a growing circle of readers.

This does not mean that books were flooding the colonies,
nor that there was a significantly large number of readers.
Not all those who bought books read them and those who
did read the books did not necessarily accept all their ideas.
Publication of books in large quantities was unknown;
indeed, very few people were literate. Some buyers used
the books for decorative purposes; some readers were outraged by what they read, if indeed it was within their grasp.
All that can be safely concluded is that a few individuals,
scattered throughout the vast empire, were strongly, visibly
affected by their reading. (How the revolutionary leaders
were influenced will be told later.) Of greater significance
is the fact that new ideas were in the air, and that some
of them were put into practice.

The ideas that were adopted, even before the independence movements began, were mostly in the realm of day-
to-day practicality—technological improvements and some
economic theories. In addition to the contributions made
by mining experts and metallurgists, and operating on a
much broader scale in promoting useful knowledge, were
the *Sociedades Económicas,* or Economic Societies. Some
were called Societies of the Friends of the Country. Modeled after similar societies in France, encouraged by the
enlightened ministers of Charles III, a considerable number of these organizations were established in Spain and

the New World. The first to be organized was the Basque Society in 1766. Within some twenty-five years there were sixty-eight functioning in Spain, with memberships varying from five hundred to five thousand; in colonial America another ten were formed between 1770 and 1822. The Societies were private, but they were endorsed and partially supported by the government. In the colonies the most influential citizens became members; there were a few peninsulars, but most were Creoles, usually from the wealthiest families.

Their methods of disseminating information included weekly discussions, publications, public meetings, and the establishment of schools and classes of instruction. Prizes were given for essays and technical drawings; models of implements and mechanical equipment were collected, displayed, and demonstrated. Seeds were imported and distributed; experiments were conducted with new plants and prizes offered for the best crops. Advice was freely offered to the government and to private individuals, and the Societies maintained a regular correspondence with one another. Agriculture, arts and crafts, and industry were the three categories stressed. The emphasis on mechanical arts and manual labor is all the more remarkable since for centuries upper-class Spaniards had had an aversion to both. A Spaniard who came to the New World for gold, glory, or God would not deign to soil his hands; nor would most Creoles.

Inspired by the Enlightenment, the Societies acted in the belief that prosperity and happiness depended upon a firm grasp and proper application of the principles of political economy (as the science of economics was then called). For example, they attacked the prevailing theory that money is wealth and deprecated the attention being given to the mining of the precious metals. An increase in commerce, they taught, would result from improvements in methods and increased production. Idleness, common among Spaniards and Creoles, was condemned on the grounds that it held back material and intellectual progress. Enlightened individuals, possessing reason and knowledge, would lead the way, setting an example and giving direction to the lower classes.

Education was to wipe out ignorance, error, and prejudice. The dissemination of ideas would change the world. Thus the first public library was opened in the New World, teachers were trained especially in the sciences and in political economy, primary schools were founded in some Indian villages, and a few vocational schools and some art schools were organized where instruction was given to whites, mestizos and Indians.

The spirit of scientific inquiry was in the air and Spanish America had its share of notable scientists. Many were native-born; some, like José Celestino Mutis (1732–1804) were peninsulars. Mutis had come to New Granada in 1761, accompanying the new viceroy as his personal physician. Mutis' extraordinary talent could not be so confined, however. He taught mathematics and astronomy at the university, where he defied the Inquisition by teaching the Copernican system. He initiated, directed, and participated in scientific investigations in New Granada that won universal acclaim. He led a corps of more than forty scholars and painters who worked for years in what came to be known as the Botanical Mission, or the Mutis Mission. They collected, classified, and made colored drawings on large plates of the flora of New Granada. Mutis' fame and methods spread to the viceroyalties of Peru and New Spain, where similar undertakings were encouraged. The Botanical Gardens in Madrid, composed in large part of contributions from the New World, became one of the finest in the world; there still survives a tremendous collection of specimens of about five thousand distinct species of herbaria (dried plants), and more than five thousand plates in full color and in black and white. The botanical library in Bogotá won the admiration of Humboldt, who considered it one of the finest in the world. Other scientists, spurred by Mutis, led field expeditions, collecting and classifying minerals, insects, and the animals of northern South America. Astronomy was greatly advanced by the construction of an observatory at Bogotá. More accurate maps of South America were drafted.

Possibly of equal stature was the distinguished Colombian scholar Francisco José de Caldas (1770–1816). Caldas had worked independently; then he corresponded with Mutis until he could at last work in Bogotá in close collaboration with his mentor. On meeting Mutis, he presented him with his life work—a huge collection that Caldas himself described as follows:

It amounts to a respectable herbarium of five or six thousand skeletons dried in the midst of the anxieties and speed of travel; two volumes of descriptions; many sketches of the most noteworthy plants done by my own hand; seeds, useful barks;

some minerals; the materials needed to draw the geographical map of the viceroyalty; what is needed for botany, for zoology; the profiles of the Andes; the geometric altitudes of the most famous peaks; more than 1,500 altitudes of various towns and mountains based on barometric observations; some animals and birds. With this material, contained in sixteen loads, I presented myself to Mutis.

Like most scientists of the time, Caldas was particularly interested in the practical consequences of research. Collection and classification were a means to an end. For example, Caldas asks his readers to turn in samples of minerals to be examined without charge. "Surrounded as we are by emeralds, amethysts, cinnabar, platinum ore, iron, copper, and lead and literally treading on gold and silver, we are poverty-stricken in the midst of riches because we do not know our own property. It is essential to know how to distinguish and recognize the worth and advantage that we could derive from nature's bounty in these favored lands." Caldas was one of the few scientists who participated in the war of independence, in the course of which he was badly wounded.

Francisco Javier Eugenio de Santa Cruz y Espejo (1747–95) was born in Ecuador of an Indian father and a mulatto mother. Espejo wrote a number of essays on literary criticism, on philosophy and social questions, on problems of public hygiene, on law, and on medicine. He was editor of Quito's first periodical, *Las Primicias de la Cultura* (1792), and director of Quito's first public library. His writings on democracy and on liberty aroused the wrath of the royal authorities so that he was several times imprisoned and died as a direct result of physical ill-treatment.

Mexico, too, was a fertile field for the development of scientific inquiry. Several newspapers dedicated to literature and science were founded there. One of the more famous periodicals was *The Literary Gazette,* edited by José Antonio Alzate y Ramírez (1729–99). Alzate wrote extensively on physics, astronomy, and the biological sciences. His scholarship was recognized abroad and he was made a corresponding member of the Academy of Science in Paris.

We have already mentioned the School of Mines in Mexico; it turned out a number of famous graduates such as the mineralogists Antonio de León y Gama (1735–1804) and Andrés del Río, the discoverer of vanadium. The School emphasized metallurgy, geology, and mining technology, but it also had a physics laboratory, a department of mathematics, and promoted the study of the new principles of chemistry.

Even before the School of Mines had been instituted, a Botanical Garden, directed by Vicente Cervantes, had been set up in 1788; an Academy of Fine Arts and the School of Medicine had been organized, all sterling examples of the growth of the scientific spirit. Humboldt was greatly impressed; he writes enthusiastically, "No city in the New World, not excepting those in the United States, has scientific establishments as large and solid as those in the Mexican capital."

In Lima, the most modern scientific thought found expression in the work of Hipólito Unánue—naturalist, meteorologist, physician, and social interpreter. His *Observations on the Climate of Lima* has been viewed as a brilliant work on human geography that anticipated modern studies on the relationship between man and his environment.

Many of these scientists were in more or less regular communication with one another, especially via the circulation of gazettes, or literary-scientific periodicals. Characteristic of the Enlightenment, the editorial concentration of the gazettes was on Progress.

What connection was there between that concept and the ideas of independence? To what degree did the men of science inculcate a desire for freedom? The evidence is scanty. Few scientists directly related their scientific investigations or their promotion of useful knowledge with thoughts of independence; Espejo was one of those few. But freedom of scientific inquiry did not seem to be limited in any serious way by imperial relations. A parallel of what had transpired in the Anglo-American colonies is handy for comparison. Did the scientific work of Benjamin Franklin or of Dr. Benjamin Rush enhance the movement of independence? Had their work been at all hindered by their status as colonists in the vast English empire? Did they participate in the revolutionary movement, as they did, because they were men of science?

None of these questions can be answered unequivocally. Those were encyclopedic minds whose interests spanned more than the physical sciences. What seems most probable is that in the revolutionary movements of the Anglo-American colonies, as well as those of Hispano-American colonies, what influenced men to act may be partly laid to science. For the same spirit of scientific inquiry that requires freedom to think may lead some men to act on broader principles of freedom. Once freedom of inquiry, however limited, becomes a reality, the whole atmosphere tends to become charged with greater possibilities. This sense of freedom as an ideal hardly arises spontaneously, but is fed in many ways over a period of time.

In all revolutions ideas play a significant role. Whether changing circumstances evoke new ideas, or inevitably accompany them, or are created by the ideas themselves is difficult to ascertain. For example, restricting trade between the colonies and the mother country was necessary and beneficial to all in the early days of settlement. But with the expansion of world commerce and an unending series of inventions in industry, navigation, and shipbuilding, what had been advantageous before became unduly restrictive and galling when commercial opportunities were multiplying. Hence came the demand for legalization of free trade, a freedom that was already being exercised illegally. Or as another illustration, one may discern behind the introduction of certain political reforms, and the demand for more, the changing economic and social structure of Europe; the supremacy of the landed aristocracy was being threatened by the rise of the new industrial bourgeoisie.

If necessity is the mother of invention, practice, if not the antecedent, is the handmaiden of theory. Nevertheless, we cannot underestimate the role of ideas, for there are no major revolutions without them. The upheavals in Spanish America were prefaced by and accompanied by revolutionary ideas—political, social and scientific—that fired the imaginations of the leaders.

❧

The expulsion of the Jesuits from Spanish America in 1767 had serious repercussions in the colonies. The Society of Jesus, founded by Ignatius Loyola, was one of the several regular orders that had set up missions and other religious institutions aimed primarily at converting the many Indians to Catholicism. The Jesuits had sent their missionary expedition to Portuguese Brazil in 1549 and the first to any of the Spanish colonies in the 1560's. Between that time and 1767 the Jesuits had constructed and successfully maintained a number of missions, particularly in frontier or border areas. In South America the Jesuits occupied extensive land in what is now Paraguay, in areas of western and southwestern Brazil, and in the interior of Argentina.

The Jesuit chain of missions in Spanish America, part of a vast international network, had accumulated tremendous wealth in the form of slaves, monasteries, convents, churches, schools, town real estate, handicraft factories, dockyards, sugar mills, warehouses, company stores, extensive farmlands, plantations, and livestock. The economic and commercial organization of the Society was huge, powerful, and extraordinarily efficient. A modern historian, Bailey W. Diffie, describes their financial organization as "the nearest thing in their age to modern chain stores and efficient manufacturers. . . . Their agricultural methods, and their skill in irrigation, were models for the time. They enjoyed the same advantages as a great modern corporation in centralized administration [and] command of large capital." They were "a state within other states, and their power transcended national boundaries." * The wealth accumulated and the religious work accomplished are even more staggering when it is realized that there were only twenty-two hundred Jesuits in Spanish America administering to seven hundred thousand Indians at the time of their expulsion.

Indians were trained in handicraft and agriculture. They were baptized, practiced Catholicism, at least superficially, and the children were given some elementary education. Indian languages, most particularly Guaraní in the Paraguay region, were mastered, given a formal structure, and books—including a grammar and religious tracts—were published in the native tongue. (To this day Guaraní, along with Spanish, is commonly spoken and written in Paraguay.) Not only did the Jesuits perform their religious duties, but they were also explorers, educators, scholars, historians. They founded colleges and libraries considered the finest in the colonies. Despite sporadic outbreaks of violence in the frontier regions, the Jesuits generally performed yeoman service in calming rebellious Indians and helping to maintain a relative peace.

Why were the Jesuits forced to leave Spanish America? There were various factors, among them the envy of the competing regular orders, the concern of royalty over the Jesuits' political power, and the covetousness of merchants and hacendados. This was a hostility that developed throughout the Catholic world. In 1759, the Marquis of Pombal (the statesman who was the effective head of state

* Bailey W. Diffie, *Latin American Civilization* (Harrisburg, Pa., 1945), pp. 585–586.

during the reign of Joseph I of Portugal) had ordered the expulsion of the Jesuits from the Portuguese empire, and in 1764 Louis XIV followed suit in France. His Bourbon cousin Charles III pursued the same drastic policy, ordering the expulsion of the Jesuits from the entire Spanish empire in 1767. Finally, the Pope—perhaps because of jealousy of the power of the Society or through pressure of the Catholic majesties—suppressed the Jesuits in 1775; the order was not to be reestablished until 1814.

A scramble for the huge Jesuit properties followed their expulsion from the colonies. Most of their material possessions went to the Crown; religious properties went to the Church and to some of the other regular orders; some of the lands and mines ultimately found their way into the hands of wealthy private citizens. The ensuing economic disruption was temporary, although it is doubtful whether the efficiency of economic operation that had been the mark of the Jesuits was restored for many decades. The evangelical work with the Indians was interrupted; their schooling was in part taken up by the Church, and the rest lapsed permanently. Higher education gained, for the ideas of the Enlightenment were being more rapidly substituted for the rigid, antiquated Jesuit doctrine. For example, secular studies such as the new natural sciences were incorporated into the currricula of the universities.

As for the twenty-two hundred Jesuits themselves, they were exiled. Though the void was quickly filled by regular and lay clergy, the dislocation was serious. Many of those deported were the sons of Creoles. The consequent breakup of families resulted in resentment that may have weakened loyalty to the monarchy. Some Jesuits in exile, notably the Peruvian Pablo Viscardo and the Chilean Juan José Godoy, fanned the embers of national consciousness through their writings. In the course of deploring their unhappy fate, they claimed loyalty not only to their previous Indian charges but also to their American homelands.

It is difficult to estimate the importance of the expulsion of the Jesuits as a factor contributing to the developing patriotic fervor. Charles III's radical act undoubtedly weakened the loyalty to the throne of some Spanish Americans, and some Indians probably lost faith in Christianity, Christians, and white men. On the other hand, some Creoles and peninsulars gained at the expense of the Society and welcomed the expulsion as a positive good. It is not likely that the expulsion was a major cause of the wars for independence; nevertheless, it must be counted among the contributing influences. Of far greater impact, however, were the American and French revolutions.

The last quarter of the eighteenth century was a period of revolutions and of a revolutionary fervor whose influence varied according to time and place. The success of the American Revolution had its immediate consequences in the French Revolution. Both influenced the course of events in Latin America. We therefore turn our attention briefly to those two momentous predecessors of the Spanish American wars for independence.

It must have been somewhat bewildering for the colonists to learn that Spain was aiding the American rebels. The

struggles for empire had led France to come to the aid of
the embattled Anglo-American revolutionists. Following
England's declaration of war upon France, Spain—as the
latter's ally—in turn declared war upon England in 1779.
To the thirteen colonies Spain lent valuable although
limited aid. New Orleans was used as a base by American
privateers who wreaked havoc upon British shipping;
British posts in West Florida were opportunely seized by
the Spaniards to prevent their use in invading the southern
colonies; American ships were outfitted, provisioned, and
operated out of Spanish ports. Of course, in giving such
support the Spanish monarchy was not endorsing the revolution or its principles. It was seeking vengeance against an
old foe and participated in the partial dismemberment of
the English empire upon the successful conclusion of the
war.

Of greater significance was the example set for Spanish
American rebels—that is, those who were already rebels
in thought and those who were to become rebels in deed.
The American colonists had conclusively proved that it
was possible to throw off imperial domination even by so
mighty a power as England. The lesson was taken to heart
by disgruntled Creoles, who could now combine the ideas
of the Enlightenment with the successful practical demon-
stration by the new United States of America.

The American Revolution was more than just a model
for the Creoles. New ideas circulated between the new
American republic and her southern neighbors. Intellectual and commercial communication, while never great,
had existed from the earliest colonial days. Now both were

enhanced. Publications of the American Philosophical Society and the writings of such prominent scientists as Benjamin Franklin, Alexander Gordon, the great botanist, and Doctors Barton, Rush, and Coxe, were read by their Latin American counterparts. Increased trade between the two Americas undoubtedly brought an additional flow of political and economic ideas via the usual channels of discourse of travelers, commercial agents, and seamen. Some individuals—a very few—endorsed such radical doctrines of democracy as are detailed in the Bill of Rights. But wealthy hacendados, cattle raisers, mine owners, and similar moneyed interests who depended upon slave and semislave labor did not relish the ideas of democracy.

Soon after the American Revolution, in 1789, the same year in which George Washington was inaugurated as first president under the newly ratified constitution, the French Revolution began. Its effect upon the course of events in Spanish America was perhaps even greater than that of the American Revolution. The ideas of the men of the Enlightenment—especially the great French *philosophes*—had their logical climax in the French Revolution. We have seen how those ideas had already begun to stir the hearts and minds of many Creoles. Now there was substantial reason for a quickening of spirits. The famous Declaration of the Rights of Man, published in the first year of the Revolution, was many times more far-reaching than the American Bill of Rights and among the most significant and pervasive documents of modern times. It had a universal appeal to men of reason. Antonio Nariño (1765–1823), one of the heroes of Colombian independence, was

among those interested by it. It was he who was daring
enough to translate and publish a copy of the Declaration
in 1795. For that defiant act, which proved to be a turning
point in his life and perhaps for the revolution in Colombia
as well, Nariño was exiled.

The arrest and execution of the French king and his
family and the many executions during the Reign of Terror
frightened many a Spanish aristocrat, both Spaniard and
Creole, enlightened or not. Not many were made of the
stuff of a Thomas Jefferson. Though he deplored the
excesses of the radical Jacobins who undoubtedly executed
some innocents along with the guilty, he commented:

> . . . the Liberty of the whole earth was dependent on the
> issue of the contest, and was ever such a prize won with so
> little innocent blood? My own affections have been deeply
> wounded by some of the martyrs to this cause, but rather
> than it should have failed I would have seen half the earth
> desolated; were there but an Adam and Eve left in every coun-
> try, and left free, it would be better than it now is.

Such revolutionary medicine was much too strong for the
average Creole. For some the French Revolution was a
source of continued inspiration, while for others it was a
harbinger of frightful events. Nevertheless, few could
ignore that a mighty monarch had been successfully challenged and that the sovereignty of the people had asserted
itself.

The official course of the Spanish monarchy was unsure,
erratic, and a source of confusion for the Spanish colonists.
At first, Charles IV had allowed himself to be guided by

intelligent ministers like Floridablanca and Aranda, who
had been impressed by the work of the French encyclopedists; but they had mixed feelings about the course of
revolutionary developments in France. When Godoy became the king's minister in 1792, the official policy of luke-
warm tolerance of the Revolution and adroit maneuvering
began to change. It changed to outright opposition when
the French king, Louis XVI, who was Charles's cousin, was
executed. Spain's ally became her enemy; war between the
two began in 1793, and ended in a humiliating defeat for
Spain in 1795. That defeat, followed by a sudden turn-
about in 1796 of Charles IV, advised or forced into making
Spain an ally of revolutionary France in her war with
England, had to contribute to the growing colonial dissatisfaction with the management of Spain's affairs. Godoy's
ministry suffered by comparison with the achievements of
his predecessors. It was common knowledge that Godoy,
designated as the "Prince of Peace" after signing the treaty
with France in 1795, was the lover of Charles's wife; although what was disturbing probably was not the fact of
the liaison itself but that it was publicly known. In addition, it became increasingly clear that Charles himself was
completely unsuited to the task of guiding his weakened
ship of state through stormy domestic and international
seas. Charles was king and as such was to be obeyed; but
as a man he was contemptible. And it is difficult for a
laughingstock to command obedience.

Explosive materials had been accumulating over a considerable period of time. In the years immediately preceding the outbreak of the Hispano-American revolutions,

the pace had been accelerated. Writing from a distant perspective, historical observers can say that an explosion was inevitable. A growing antagonism between peninsulars and Creoles, the emergence of nationalist feelings, the expulsion of the Jesuits, the consequences of the political and economic reforms under the Spanish Bourbons, the inept rule of Charles IV, a growing inefficiency of colonial administration, the examples set by the American and French revolutions, and the profound effects of the Enlightenment and its manifold ramifications—all this constituted the explosive material which waited to be set off by some capricious spark. The fuse was lit with the invasion of Spain by Napoleon in 1807.

~~~

Napoleon's ambitious plans for a European empire brought him to the conclusion that he had to safeguard France from possible attack by Spain, whose military potential was not to be underestimated. Toward the close of 1807 Napoleon hatched a cunning plan. He was aware of growing internal dissension in Spain, where one faction, dissatisfied with Charles IV and his minister Godoy, was supporting the claims of Ferdinand, Charles's son, to the throne. After dispatching General Junot at the head of a French military force into northern Spain, Napoleon invited Charles and Ferdinand to Bayonne, in southern France. After listening to the arguments of both, he secured their abdications and clapped both in jail. Increasing the French forces invading Spain with the aim of completely subjugating that unhappy land, Napoleon boldly announced that his brother Joseph was to be installed as king of Spain. Napoleon deluded himself that in this way he would not be troubled by his southern neighbor and would therefore be able to concentrate his energies elsewhere in Europe.

The French emperor's plans were rudely upset. Sporadic, unofficial, unorganized, but determined armed resistance to the French proved exceedingly nettlesome from the beginning. Matters got out of hand immediately following an extraordinary event; on May 2, 1808—a date still commemorated in Spain as perhaps her finest hour—a popular uprising began in Madrid, much to the angry consternation of Joseph and to the *afrancesados* (Spaniards servilely supporting the French). Other popular uprisings followed in occupied regions of Spain, enthusiastically supported by patriotic demonstrations in the as yet unoccupied territory. For Napoleon this was the beginning of the Peninsular War; for the Spaniards it was the beginning of a war of independence that was in turn to trigger the wars of independence in the Americas.

The people of Spain proved absolutely fearless. The authorities—that is, the audiencias and the Council of Castile—had been afraid to defy Napoleon. But the people had no such fears and were ready to fight whether the constituted authorities endorsed their actions or not. The people were infuriated because the soil of Spain was being violated by the hated French, whose conduct in Spain, like that of most invading armies, was incredibly brutal. Goya's famous etchings, *The Disasters of War*, depict far more vividly than any written description the gruesome horrors accompanying an army of occupation. The populace was also indignant at the usurpation of their sovereignty by the peremptory installation of a new king of Spain.

The spontaneous uprisings and guerrilla activities became better organized as new leaders were found. In each of the provinces a revolutionary junta was created; subsequently a Central Junta was established that was to provide over-all leadership for the popular resistance.

The events in Spain had their repercussions in the overseas colonies. For decades Spanish Americans had been expected to follow unquestioningly the many and tortuous changes of Spain's foreign policies. We have already noted the changes consequent upon the French Revolution. There had been the peculiar somersault of first waging war against France in 1793, then—after a short-lived peace —joining with France in war against England. Now, in 1808, a truly strange series of events began to unfold. A complex dilemma confronted Spaniards overseas. Were the royal appointees—the officials of the colonial audiencias, the intendants, the viceroys, and others—to function on behalf of Ferdinand, the claimant to the throne, or Joseph, *de facto* king of Spain? To whom did the Creoles owe their loyalty? The constituted authorities in Spain had been deposed or were no longer recognized by the people; now ruling were juntas representing theoretically the will of the people. In Seville, the Central Junta was acting as the government heading a popular rebellion. Should the colonists heed the Junta and recognize it as genuinely representing Ferdinand VII? Should the people be supported in their revolt against Napoleon? How were the emissaries of Joseph to be received? To whom should revenue be given? Just as in Spain, the loyalties of men in the colonies were pulled in various directions. Whatever unanimity may have existed before was now ended.

Intimately related to those practical matters was the question of a country's sovereignty. For decades there had been discussion about whether sovereignty rested with the monarch or with the people. Now political theory was thrust upon the historical stage at a time when the decision would have immediate practical consequences. The endless intellectual debates were to be dramatically transformed into physical combats.

CHAPTER THREE

The Revolution in New Spain

THE REVOLUTIONS IN THE SPANISH POSSES-
sions in the New World took place almost simultaneously,
yet there was little connection among the several revolts
in distinct areas of the overseas empire. The revolution
in New Spain seemed to have no intimate relationship
with the other revolutions in South America, and the outbreaks in the three southern viceroyalties had minimal
influence upon one another initially. What is significant
is that the same set of causes operated independently in
diverse regions, each of which produced the leaders they
needed to achieve their goals.

Once begun, however, the rebellions took their several
courses, moving independently of one another. Differences
in geographic, political, economic, and social conditions,
in ethnic composition, and in the strength of the royalist
forces present affected the precise character of the revolu-

tionary movements. Therefore it is necessary to treat them separately. The first liberation movement to be considered is that in New Spain, but the reader must bear in mind that similar developments were occurring in South America.

The revolution in New Spain went through several phases. The first, beginning in September of 1810, ended with the execution of its leader, Miguel Hidalgo; the second ended just as tragically with the execution of the next of the great revolutionary figures, José Morelos. A third phase of prolonged guerrilla warfare merged into a brief but conclusive struggle from which Mexico emerged as an independent nation in 1821.

༄

The revolutionary currents in Spanish America evolved as movements for independence. The revolutions did not have democratic goals; although a few participants had democratic aspirations, their counsel did not prevail. Only the first phase of the revolution in New Spain espoused humanitarian and democratic ideals. In the ultimate phase of the struggle, those ideals were suppressed by mundane, narrow interests.

The heart of New Spain was the area now known as Mexico. The borderlands, the area north of the Rio Grande River, were sparsely settled and, at the time, of little economic value. Nor did the Central American part of the viceroyalty approach the economic importance of Mexico. Her wonderfully fertile soils, rich mineral deposits (especially the inexhaustible silver mines), the huge cattle industry, and the relatively large population all combined to make Mexico the most important portion of New Spain. Mexico was the center of a revolutionary fervor that was absent or relatively insignificant in the rest of the vast subempire.

When the news reached Mexico that Napoleon had compelled the abdication of Charles, imprisoned his son Ferdinand, and boldly installed Joseph Bonaparte as king of Spain, wild confusion resulted. To most, it was unthinkable to pledge allegiance to the usurper. What had previously been faint stirrings for independence became significant currents. Promotion of ideas and simple agitation were rapidly transformed into action. Creoles argued that, since the Spanish Crown was in involuntary exile, all loyal to Ferdinand VII should follow the model that had been set by Spanish patriots in the peninsula, who had set up a Central Junta in Seville to rule in the name of the imprisoned Spanish king and to act as the center of resistance to the French invaders. Some Creoles proposed that Mexicans establish their own junta to rule in the name of Ferdinand. The peninsulars favored maintenance of the existing authorities acting in loyal support of the Spanish junta. It was quite peculiar that the extremely conservative peninsulars, joined by some conservative, wealthy, Creoles (especially first-generation Americans), should support the revolutionary junta in Spain. But it seemed the lesser of two evils; they feared their power would be usurped if the liberal Creoles gained control by establishing a Mexican junta.

Each faction sought to make use of an unusual opportunity to take over the government. At a joint meeting of the audiencia and the cabildo of Mexico City, opposite solutions were proposed. The Creoles found surprising support from the viceroy, José de Iturrigaray, a former military commander who had grown rich through the sale of public offices. Now he had a bigger prize in view. He thought that, with the aid of the Creole majority, he could become dictator of a Mexico that would eventually sever its ties completely with imperial Spain.

The Spaniards, alarmed at this turn of events, plotted to depose the viceroy. Leadership was entrusted to a wealthy Spanish sugar grower, Don Gabriel Yermo. A simple plan was put into operation. The palace guards were bribed, and very early in the morning of September 14, 1808, a small group of conspirators stealthily entered the viceregal palace. Iturrigaray was arrested and ultimately deported to Spain. In his place, the audiencia appointed General Pedro de Garibay, a senile old man who subordinated himself completely to the audiencia. In overthrowing the viceroy, the audiencia had destroyed basic principles of authority, for the court had taken upon itself a right that was solely that of the king. For many decades thereafter this coup d'état served as a model for instituting governmental changes in Mexico. It had an immediate effect upon the Creole insurgents, who lost all respect for a viceroyalty that could be so easily deposed.

Popular demonstrations against the new administration were quickly and easily suppressed by loyal troops; they unquestioningly obeyed an officer caste whose upper ranks were almost exclusively Spanish. The superior military forces compelled a limited course of action; the discon-

tented increased clandestine activities, particularly through
the medium of "literary" clubs and other secret societies.
The winds of revolution were blowing more strongly, not
only in the viceregal capital, but also in several areas of
the Mexican heartland. Some of the lessons of the French
Revolution were eagerly seized upon by infuriated Creoles
who were more than willing to heed the advice of French
exiles, some of whom were Napoleon's agents. The wily
French Emperor hoped to disrupt the Spanish empire and
perhaps thought of annexing a part of it. Therefore his
agents sowed the ideas of nationalism and liberalism
among the frustrated Creoles.

For about two years the revolution simmered. What
set it boiling was the kind of extraordinary coincidence
that accompanies complicated events. Revolutions are
never tidy affairs. Among the several plots was the one
being hatched by the leaders of the literary and social
club of Querétaro. Among the chief conspirators of the
club were Don Miguel Hidalgo y Costilla, an obscure
village priest, and Ignacio Allende, a young, moderately
wealthy Creole landowner.

⟨⟩

Father Hidalgo's early career held much promise until he
incurred the disfavor of the Inquisition. He had received
the degree of bachelor of arts in 1770 from the University
of Mexico and in 1773 the degree of sacred theology. He
became a teacher at the College of San Nicolás, and after
showing his brilliance in winning an academic prize
awarded by the dean of the college, he was made rector in

1791. He relinquished that post in order to serve as curate in small villages. In 1800 he was denounced by several persons to the Holy Office on a number of counts. It was alleged, among other charges, that he disparaged several popes, that he doubted the virginity of the Christ Mother, that he did not consider fornication to be a sin, that he himself had committed that sin (he had, in fact, fathered several children), and in general was dissolute and immoral in his daily conduct. His denouncers also accused him of being a lover of French liberty and of being opposed to the monarchical form of government. No formal trial was conducted, but in 1803 Hidalgo was relegated to serving as priest in the tiny village of Dolores, in the province of Guanajuato.

There, Hidalgo violated the letter and the spirit of Spanish law. Whether it was simply a humanitarian or a revolutionary impulse, the curate undertook to train Indians in various skills. Although it had been expressly forbidden to practice sericulture, Hidalgo planted a number of mulberry trees for the culture of the silkworm. He taught the Indians how to plant grape vines and to engage in a number of other agricultural enterprises unfamiliar to them. The Indians were avid students of a number of industrial skills such as carpentering, blacksmithing, pottery and brick making, and leather tanning. Such practical activities, taught at the expense of priestly duties, did not endear Hidalgo to the authorities in Mexico City. Yet he did gain the favor of a number of prominent individuals in the province.

Hidalgo's chief co-conspirator was Ignacio Allende, who,

along with some fellow Creole army officers, a petty official in the post office at Querétaro, and other leaders, had set October 1 (1810) for an uprising aimed specifically at eliminating the Spanish administration. Posters had been prepared reading: "Americans, be alert and do not be deceived. Today all the gachupines are to be killed . . ."

Despite the extreme caution with which the plotters operated, detailed information was presented to the viceroy on September 11. Apparently the group had been under surveillance for some time, and it seems quite likely that a traitor had penetrated their ranks. Fortunately for the conspirators, they learned that they had been betrayed and that all the leaders were to be arrested. On the night of Saturday, September 15, Captain Aldama, one of the conspirators, started out on horse from San Miguel el Grande; early on Sunday morning, he galloped into Dolores, where he awoke the startled priest. A hurried conference led to a hasty decision. Hidalgo had determined to commence the revolution immediately, no matter how ill-prepared.

Messengers were dispatched to gather cached arms, while the fifty-seven-year-old minor cleric, accompanied by Allende and some trusted aides, proceeded to the church in the main plaza. A furious bellringing summoned the startled populace, but not to Sunday mass. Instead the assembled Indians listened to Hidalgo's impassioned speech exhorting them to rebel. Eagerly they took up their beloved curate's cry at the conclusion of his speech: "Long live America! Long live religion! Down with bad government!" (The scene is reenacted on the night of every September 15–16 in the great square in Mexico City, when the President thus concludes the ceremonies celebrating Independence Day.) The enthusiastic Indians added "Death to the gachupines!" and, later in the day, still another slogan, "Long live our Virgin of Guadalupe!" Hidalgo's rousing cry became the battle cry of the Revolution, the *Grito de Dolores*.

In a matter of hours, the Indians prepared to do battle armed with machetes, bows and arrows, stones, clubs, lances, and a few firearms. Behind their priest-leader, the spontaneously created army of liberation sallied forth, flushed with optimism and with thoughts of revenge.

The liberation army had the advantages of surprise and superior numbers. As it proceeded from village to village, volunteers quickly joined what became a poorly organized mob, much to the chagrin of seasoned military men like Allende. But Hidalgo was an inspired leader who was able to bind together some 50,000 Indians, mestizos, and a few Creoles. It was a rag-tail army, equipped with most primitive weapons, living off the country, raiding haciendas to obtain food and other provisions as well as to recruit herdsmen and laborers. There was little discipline; rioting, looting, and almost senseless attacks against peninsulars and even Creoles horrified the leaders, who were unable to stem the flood so suddenly unleashed. The long pent-up hatred of the Indians found release in violent revenge. "Death to the gachupines!" was a more significant rallying cry for the Indians than abstract notions of government or of independence from Spain. As they saw it, the enemy was not the representative of a distant land but the im-

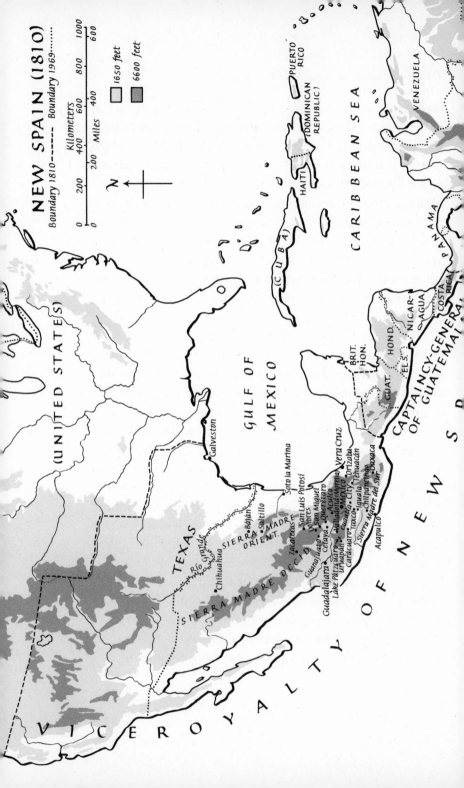

NEW SPAIN (1810)

Boundary 1810 ------
Boundary 1969 ········

Kilometers
0   200   400   600   800   1000

Miles
0   200   400   600

1650 feet
6600 feet

N

(UNITED STATES)

GULF OF MEXICO

Galveston

TEXAS

Río Grande

Chihuahua

SIERRA MADRE OCCID.

SIERRA MADRE ORIENT.

Béjan · Saltillo

Zacatecas

Soto la Marina

San Luis Potosí

Dolores

San Miguel

Querétaro

Guanajuato

Celaya

Guadalajara

Lake Pátzcuaro

Uruapan

Carácuaro

Valladolid (Morelia)

Acuico

Guada... MEXICO CITY

Taxco

Iguala

Tehuacán

Chilpancingo

Sierra Madre del Sur

Acapulco

Vera Cruz

Orizaba

Oaxaca

CUBA

Puerto Rico

Haiti

(Dominican Republic)

CARIBBEAN SEA

Venezuela

Panama

Costa Rica

Nicaragua

Hond.

Brit. Hon.

Guat.

Els.

CAPTAINCY-GENERAL OF GUATEMALA

VICEROYALTY OF NEW S...

mediate exploiter whom they knew firsthand and upon whom they could wreak revenge in the only way meaningful to them.

The rebel army, swollen after initial victories at San Miguel and Celaya, descended upon Guanajuato, capital of the intendancy of the same name. News of the approaching insurgents had reached the intendant, Juan Antonio Riaño, a few days before. He decided to concentrate the defense behind the massive walls of a large, fortress-like granary, the Alhóndiga de Granaditos. Some five hundred gachupines and a few Creoles—men, women, and children —barricaded themselves in the well-provisioned Alhóndiga. The mass of citizenry—about sixty-six thousand—were left to fend for themselves.

Most of the inhabitants joined Hidalgo's army. The miners of Guanajuato, who flocked to Hidalgo's banner, proved to be the key in overcoming the impregnability of the Alhóndiga. A spirited defense, in the course of which two thousand insurgents were killed, ended after five hours; the miners heroically placed charges of dynamite which opened breaches in the walls at the same time that the huge, wooden doors were set aflame with pine torches. Thousands of Indians entered the granary; about three hundred defenders were killed; the rest were taken prisoner.

The fall of the granary on September 28 was followed by the sack of the city. Despite the attempts of Hidalgo and other leaders to prevent it, the Indians and the town's inhabitants looted and wantonly destroyed property in an orgy that lasted two days. The excesses at Guanajuato may be attributed in part to Hidalgo's weak leadership, but one cannot ignore that the Spanish colonial system had reaped its own whirlwind. Centuries of oppression, memories of the robbery and the exploitation of the lands of their ancestors undoubtedly drove the Indians to exact revenge whenever the opportunity was offered them. Hidalgo and his colleagues had not meant to foment class warfare, but once they had set the machinery of revolution into motion, it was impossible to limit its conduct to suit simple, high moralistic, and abstract political aims.

꩜

The plan of the revolution was vague. Two of the fundamental, declared aims of Hidalgo—to eliminate the foreign oppressor and to abolish Negro slavery—were explicit enough. Distribution of land to the Indians and creation of a new government were also declared purposes of the revolution, but they were never concretely formulated.

No machinery was created to institute a government to replace the colonial administration; no concrete plans were presented. The appeal to the people was made on the broadest grounds, as is evident in the manifesto which Hidalgo issued December 15, 1810. Some excerpts follow:

Mexicans, let us break the bonds of ignominy with which we have been so long bound! To break these bonds we need only to unite. If we do not fight among ourselves, the war will be terminated, and our rights will be saved. Let us then unite all those persons who have been born on this happy soil; let us consider as strangers and as enemies of our prerogatives all persons who are not Mexicans. Let us establish a congress composed of representatives of all the cities, towns, and villages of this country. The principal object of that congress will be to maintain our holy religion and to frame wise and beneficent laws adapted to the circumstances of each community. Our lawmakers will rule us with the tenderness of parents. They will treat us like brothers; they will banish poverty; they will check the devastation of the kingdom and the exportation of its money; they will encourage the arts; and they will cause industry to revive. We shall make free use of the richest productions of our fertile soil; and, in the course of a few years, the Mexicans will enjoy all the delights which the sovereign author of nature has bestowed upon this vast continent.

Following the success at Guanajuato, Hidalgo and his nondescript army proceeded to Valladolid, where headquarters were established and a rudimentary executive group was formed. Hidalgo assumed the title of Generalissimo and distributed lesser commands to experienced officers. In the meantime the insurrection spread through northern, western, and southern Mexico, where José Morelos, commissioned by Hidalgo, was conducting a vigorous campaign.

Nominally the insurgent leaders declared for Ferdinand VII. "Death to the gachupines!" was the rallying cry. Leaders of a sort came forward in towns and villages to head undisciplined guerrilla bands that raided and looted not only the haciendas of peninsulars but those of Creoles as well. Merchant caravans and silver trains were particularly rewarding prizes. The leaders included village priests, muleteers, *rancheros* (small farmers), bandits, and smugglers. One town after another fell into rebel hands: in Zacatecas there was a spontaneous uprising of the people;

in San Luis Potosí, friar Herrara, a friend of Hidalgo's, led a successful uprising; Saltillo was taken by troops led by Jiménez, a fellow officer of Allende. Success was contagious. Officials in Nuevo León and in Texas proclaimed their allegiance to Hidalgo.

The authorities in Mexico City and peninsulars everywhere were frightened. So were the Creoles, for they were alienated by the excesses of the Indians and by Hidalgo's pledges to abolish the customary tribute from Indians and to restore their lands. Creole hatred of the gachupines became subordinate to their desire to protect their own interests, which were so obviously threatened by the Hidalgo program. Any struggle for independence in which the Creoles might engage did not include a program of social, political, and economic democracy. They hastened to staff the army being organized by Viceroy Venegas, who had arrived in Vera Cruz in late August and reached Mexico City on September 14, some thirty-six hours before the Grito de Dolores sparked the rebellion.

The difficulties plaguing Venegas, so unceremoniously thrust into the midst of revolution, were complicated by the fact that the military forces he could count on were scattered throughout distant provincial towns. To gather an army large enough to meet Hidalgo's rapidly growing tens of thousands was a formidable task. Venegas had to defend the capital, apportion troops to protect the large towns, and still suppress the guerrilla bands that were springing up throughout Mexico. All of this was to be accomplished with no more than 28,000 men and officers, whereas Hidalgo's main force alone numbered some sixty thousand by mid-October and toward the end of the month had swelled to eighty thousand.

The Spaniards employed other weapons besides force to weaken the revolutionary cause. Each rebel leader had a price of ten thousand pesos upon his head. An edict of excommunication was promulgated against Hidalgo. The Indians were absolved from paying tribute and Venegas made vague promises to adopt laws to ameliorate long-standing economic and social abuses. Lastly, the Creoles were asked to defend the king, religion, and themselves against the angry mobs.

ᓚᔓ

At Valladolid Hidalgo reorganized the army with the efficient aid of Allende and other experienced military leaders. Plans were put into execution to invade the capital. The first crucial test came when the revolutionary force, comprising some eighty regiments of one thousand each, were confronted by royalist forces numbering a mere eighteen hundred. Lieutenant Colonel Torcuato Trujillo, the royalist commander, had set up a strong defense on a mountain pass overlooking the fertile Valley of Mexico, with Mexico City at the distant eastern end. The pass was known as Monte de Las Cruces (Mount of the Crosses), site of numerous crosses standing lonely vigil over the remains of the bandits who had been hanged and buried there. Amid the forests of oak and pine, Trujillo awaited the onslaught of his numerically superior enemy. With well-armed and seasoned men, he felt confident, but he was cautious enough to place his command post on the very summit of a mountain. There he could survey the forthcoming battle and conveniently retreat should such drastic action prove expedient.

Hidalgo had given himself the title of Generalissimo, but he lacked military training and had no predilection for military affairs. Although he accepted full responsibility, he relied heavily on the capable Allende and his fellow officers. Their plan of attack placed a premium on an assault force of several thousands of the best troops, yet many untrained Indians played a vanguard role in the attack on the heights of Las Cruces. The royalists were unable to cope with the overwhelming numbers of the rebels. After a few hours of carnage, Trujillo fled into the valley and soon reached the capital. Hidalgo's first major battle had been won, but at a frightful cost. The small royalist force had killed and wounded at least two thousand insurgents while itself suffering losses of only several hundred.

Trujillo's report of victory deceived no one, least of all the viceroy, whose fear approached hysteria. His most capable commander, Félix María Calleja, was occupied in and near Querétaro. The forces in the capital alone might not be able to hold off the tens of thousands of rebels. Either fear or sagacity or both induced Venegas to have recourse to a psychological maneuver. Inasmuch as Hidalgo's movement was inspired by the Virgin of Guadalupe, Venegas sought to counteract that religious influence by investing the Virgin of Los Remedios as the religious symbol of the royalist forces. The Virgin was a wooden image brought by a Spaniard several centuries before. It reposed in a church in a hamlet just a few miles outside

Mexico City. Many miracles had been attributed to it, and now it was called upon to effect another. Venegas ordered the holy image removed to the cathedral in Mexico. The viceroy and his generals kneeled in obeisance and prayer, calling upon the Virgin to protect the city and its inhabitants and naming the image as Captain-General of the Spanish forces.

The contrasting symbolism of the Virgin of Guadalupe pitted against the Virgin of Los Remedios took on historical significance. The site of the Virgin of Guadalupe had been consecrated because an Indian had allegedly witnessed a miracle there. The Virgin of Los Remedios had been consecrated originally because of an alleged miracle performed in Spain prior to the statue's transfer to New Spain. The one Virgin was the symbol and inspirer of the Indians, whereas the other was the revered symbol of the gachupines. The class war unleashed by Hidalgo now found its religious expression: the Virgin of Guadalupe against the Virgin of Los Remedios; the Virgin of the oppressed opposed to the Virgin of the oppressors; Indian versus gachupín.

Naturally Venegas could count on the Catholic hierarchy, which, in addition to lending moral support and, specifically, economic aid, had excommunicated Father Hidalgo, the most severe punishment that could be inflicted upon a devout Catholic. The edict issued by the Holy Office also reiterated the charges that had been leveled against Hidalgo nine years before; furthermore it threatened with fines, excommunication, and other severe penalties anyone who supported Hidalgo or the revolution.

The insurgents' victory at Las Cruces had a mixed effect upon the victors. The heavy losses weakened morale, and many Indians deserted; but that loss was tempered by the fact of victory over the royalists, especially since Trujillo had fled. Allende and his fellow officers were quite confident that the defenses of the capital could be overcome and that complete victory was in their grasp. Hidalgo, perhaps discouraged by the piles of bodies strewn for miles along the mountainside, or estimating that the morale of the Indians had suffered too serious a blow, or because he believed that the defenses of the capital might prove too strong to be surmounted by his undisciplined and poorly equipped Indians, came to an opposite conclusion. At first the curate delayed, apparently considering for three days the advisability of proceeding to the capital, clearly visible from the summit of Las Cruces. It was tantalizing. Just a few hours away stood the magnificent prize whose conquest could mean the realization of his dreams. But on November 3 Hidalgo, against the wishes of his officers, decided to retreat, moving in the direction of Querétaro.

In Querétaro, Calleja learned of the movement of Hidalgo's forces. Calleja, an extremely capable commander, already victorious in suppressing the revolt in and near Querétaro, was anxious to come to grips with the main body of revolutionists. With some 7,000 well-disciplined troops, he intercepted the *hidalguistas* at Aculco. Allende and Hidalgo, realizing that their demoralized and reduced force of 40,000 might be a poor match for Calleja's men, avoided a direct confrontation and attempted a strategic retreat while maintaining what was no more than a rearguard action. The retreat turned into a rout, with Hidalgo and the other leaders barely escaping. During the precipitate retreat Hidalgo's dispirited army was further weakened by wholesale desertions and by growing dissension between Hidalgo and his officers. Finally it was decided to split the forces, Allende proceeding to Guanajuato and Hidalgo to Valladolid.

At Guanajuato, Allende arranged for the manufacture of artillery and other weapons, and reorganized and drilled his men in an attempt to create a disciplined army. At Valladolid, Hidalgo, still retaining his tremendous popular appeal, was able to regroup an army of 7,000, with which he moved to Guadalajara, chief city in western Mexico. That city had already capitulated to José Antonio Torres, a gifted peasant leader and friend of Hidalgo's. A huge reception arranged by Torres encouraged Hidalgo, and news of triumphant rebellions in the north and of Morelos' continued minor victories in the south gave him additional hope. At this moment Hidalgo could not know that the high point of his revolutionary leadership had been reached with the Pyrrhic victory at Las Cruces. On the contrary, he was still Generalíssimo of the Revolution, which he believed would achieve ultimate victory soon.

～

Hidalgo spent the next two months in reorganizing the army and in attempting to establish a national government. The latter consisted of a ministry of two and the replacement of royalist judges in the audiencia with revolutionaries. Hoping to obtain aid from the United States,

Hidalgo sent an envoy with plenipotentiary powers. The envoy, a botanist named Pacuasio Ortiz de Letona, was captured, and committed suicide while awaiting execution in Mexico City.

Most important of Hidalgo's efforts at creating a national government was the contents of a series of decrees providing for important social reforms. On November 29, he decreed the abolition of Negro slavery, one of the first attempts in the Western Hemisphere to end that infamous institution. The effects, like those of Lincoln's Emancipation Proclamation fifty-two years later, were primarily moral and psychological. Hidalgo had no real means of enforcing such an edict, since he exercised limited control over a very small part of the country. The same is true for the other humanitarian reforms Hidalgo tried to institute: the abolition of tribute paid by Indians to their masters (also in the decree of November 29), and, in the decree of December 5, the provision that land belonging to the Indian communities should be cultivated by the Indians for their own benefit.

Until this time Hidalgo's aim of achieving independence had been concealed behind declarations of allegiance to Ferdinand VII. However, the first insurgent newspaper, *El Despertador Americano*, edited by the curate Francisco Severo Maldonado, published the following statement by Hidalgo: "The entire nation has declared for independence. . . . The nation which was so long lethargic suddenly awakes from its sleep at the sweet voice of liberty." As each issue appeared, the declarations for independence were reiterated, along with arguments justifying a complete break with Spain. Self-government was declared a divine right and justified further by the assertion that an oppressed people had the right to liberate itself from "an arbitrary and tyrannical government." The American and French revolutions were bearing new fruit.

Meanwhile Calleja was not wasting time, and he drove Allende out of Guanajuato with comparative ease. His approach triggered a series of atrocities in that hapless city. Undisciplined rebels, partly in retaliation against harsh measures known to have been employed by Calleja's men, slaughtered over a hundred prisoners still being held in the Alhóndiga. When Calleja's forces finally arrived, their brutality surpassed that of the rebels; they showed no mercy either to captured rebels or toward inhabitants denounced as supporters of the Revolution. Allende fled with a remnant of loyal men and reached Guadalajara on December 12. Hidalgo put him in charge of reorganizing and outfitting the army, now grown once again to huge proportions in response to Hidalgo's fervent appeals.

Against Allende's advice, Hidalgo resolved to risk all on one battle, for it was known that Calleja was moving rapidly to Guadalajara. Hidalgo's confidence affected the troops; they marched proudly behind their beautifully uniformed leader mounted on a splendid charger. About thirty miles east of Guadalajara the officers disposed their troops on several hills overlooking the Calderón river and the bridge that spanned it. The next day, January 17, 1811, the two armies clashed. Against Hidalgo's seventy to seventy-five thousand men, Calleja led six thousand. Would superiority of numbers overcome superiority of discipline, training, and equipment?

For six hours the battle raged, its outcome in doubt

until a strange and exceedingly fateful accident. A chance shot from the royalist artillery hit an ammunition wagon. The ensuing explosion, besides killing and wounding many insurgents, set fire to the parched, thick grass and spread with amazing rapidity. The combination of wind and dry grass soon created an inferno of fire and smoke, and the men panicked. Thousands fled, thousands were killed, and thousands surrendered. The battle was suddenly over. Hidalgo had gambled and lost.

Some remnants of the rebel army and all the leaders were able to retreat to a hacienda at Pabellón. Allende compelled Hidalgo to yield his position as commander of the army, although the priest was to retain nominal leadership of the Revolution. The new military chief decided on a new course of action. In the north, insurgent chiefs were still victorious. A new army would be organized there. That might prove especially advantageous, for Allende believed he could obtain the support of the United States, whose territory bordered Mexico's northeastern provinces. Ignacio Aldama was dispatched to the United States with enough money to recruit thirty thousand men.

This part of the plan came to an abrupt, unhappy end. Aldama was captured in Texas by a counterrevolutionist, Manuel Zambrano, who proclaimed himself ruler of Texas and the neighboring province of Coahuila. The insurgents in Texas were suddenly thrust out of power and imprisoned gachupines restored to liberty. Zambrano received unexpected aid from a Colonel Ignacio Elizondo, who now decided to betray the cause in which he had professed belief. His request for promotion to lieutenant general had been denied by Allende, and the frustrated colonel seized the moment for personal revenge.

Zambrano endorsed Elizondo's plan to set an ambush for the revolutionary troops approaching the wells at Baján. Hidalgo and Allende quite unsuspectingly rode into the trap. A feeble effort at resistance, in the course of which Allende's son was killed, was quickly overcome. The bulk of the insurgent forces escaped and dispersed, leaderless. The Hidalgo revolt was finished.

∿

Hidalgo and the other leaders were brought to Chihuahua and imprisoned while they awaited military trial; after that the priest was to undergo an ecclesiastical trial as well. For two weeks Hidalgo pondered his fate and reviewed his past before the military interrogation began. A court of nine judges, six of whom were Creoles and three gachupines, headed by the specially commissioned Judge Angel Abella, put the defendants through an arduous interrogation. Hidalgo courageously attempted to take sole responsibility for the leadership of the Revolution and for any crimes allegedly committed in the course of exercising it. Nevertheless, all but one of the defendants were unanimously condemned to be shot in the back.

On May 18 Hidalgo wrote a paper in which he recanted; the weeks of incarceration and the rigors of the interrogation may account in part for Hidalgo's extraordinary action. The paper and other aspects of his recorded testimony indicate that he had concluded that the revolt was a mistake, that he had deviated from Catholic dogma, that he had been responsible for the mob's wanton vengeance in murdering peninsulars, and that dictatorship would have been an inevitable result of his movement.

The authenticity of the written confession has been placed in doubt by many historians, but the recorded trial testimony, if it is reliable, seems to corroborate that Hidalgo had sincerely denounced the Revolution. Perhaps mental torture had induced him to recant. Perhaps his devotion to Catholicism and an intense desire to make peace with his God motivated this radical change of heart. The complete truth is obscured in the partisan, incomplete records of the past.

Before the military court could sentence Hidalgo, he had to be tried before an ecclesiastical court. That institution endorsed the depositions sent by Judge Abella and further ordered the priest's defrocking. The morning of July 30, Hidalgo was led to the site of execution, tied to the seat, and—unlike his fellow conspirators—was permitted to face the firing squad. Two volleys put an end to the Father of Mexican Independence. But he had set into motion (with the historic Grito de Dolores) a cause that did not die with him.

Though no cause can be successful without great leaders, no great leadership is likely without a worthy cause. Leaders may come and go, but a genuine cause will continue, producing leaders to meet changing situations. After the battle of Las Cruces, the movement led by Hidalgo continued towards its eventual disintegration. However, Hidalgo's revolt was but a part, although a very important part, of a revolutionary movement that was infinitely more significant than the role played by any one of its leaders. Hidalgo's death ended the first phase of the independence movement. Yet the second phase had begun, so to speak, even before the first was so dramatically terminated. For many months, since October of 1810, the independence movement was developing in southern Mexico under the brilliant leadership of José María Morelos.

When the royalists placed the heads of Hidalgo and his colleagues on the posts of the Alhóndiga in Guanajuato, it was thought they would serve as both reminder and epitaph. The echoes of the Grito de Dolores were to have more profound reverberations.

At the top of a peak on the island of Janitzio in Lake Pátzcuaro rests a gigantic statue of José Morelos. The statue, overlooking the area in which Morelos had lived and worked prior to his revolutionary activities, is larger than the Statue of Liberty standing vigil on its smaller island in New York harbor. The New York statue is an idealized representation of Liberty. The statue in Janitzio is a representation of the Mexican who was a living apostle of liberty. The statue is immense; Morelos was squat, not quite five feet. Yet the sculptor has caught the spirit and grandeur of one of Mexico's illustrious heroes. Lázaro Cárdenas, President of Mexico (1934–40), expressed the feelings of all Mexicans in ordering the erection of so majestic a monument.

Morelos was born on September 30, 1765, near the city of Valladolid, now known as Morelia in honor of the liberator. His parents were a poor carpenter and the daughter of the local schoolmaster. His childhood was spent as a muleteer, and as a young adult he served a short time as cowhand. In 1790 he began to study for the priesthood in response to the urging of his widowed mother. He was awarded the bachelor of arts in 1795 from San Nicolás Obispo, the same college Hidalgo had attended earlier and where he was now serving as rector. After his ordination Morelos served as an impoverished priest in obscure parishes populated principally by Indians and mestizos.

Morelos was the curate of Carácuaro when the Revolution broke out. He did not learn of it for several weeks and took no action until a few days after he had been ordered by Bishop Manuel Abad y Queipo to publish the October 13 ban of excommunication against Hidalgo and his supporters. It may have been curiosity which impelled Morelos to seek an interview with the priest who had been rector at San Nicolás. Perhaps the curiosity was stirred by resentment against his impecunious status as a village priest, a resentment further heightened by the discrimination practiced against a mestizo. The exact motives for Morelos' sudden decision to enter into the revolutionary struggle are not known. On October 20, in Indaparapeo, after a brief interview with Hidalgo, Morelos acccepted the commission offered him as *lugar-teniente* (lieutenant) in the south. He was instructed to raise troops there, collect arms, reorganize the local governments, capture Europeans, deport their families, and confiscate their property. The principal military objective was to capture the important port of Acapulco on the Pacific coast. Morelos, convinced by his former rector that the cause was just, accepted the commission without hesitation.

He returned to his curate where he recruited about twenty-five men and set out to fulfill the herculean task confronting him. In the course of a slow march to the Pacific coast, his small band grew and at the same time was able to capture one village after another. Within a few weeks Morelos commanded a force of a few thousand. Not long after these early military victories, Morelos issued, on November 10, a most important social document. Anticipating by a few weeks Hidalgo's famous decree on social reforms, Morelos boldly proclaimed the abolition of Indian tribute, slavery, and the caste system. As was the case with Hidalgo's social legislation, the most important immediate consequence of this proclamation was that the oppressed were ready to give Morelos maximum support. Especially significant was Morelos' denunciation of the caste system. He proclaimed that there were no longer to be any disparaging distinctions of mulatto, mestizo, Creole and so on, but that all inhabitants except Europeans were to be known as Americans. That egalitarian declaration, repeated several times during the next years, earned him the undying hatred of every conservative element in Mexico.

For almost six months Morelos besieged Acapulco unsuccessfully. He and his men gained valuable military experience, however, from the many skirmishes and minor engagements. After learning of Hidalgo's capture, Morelos decided upon a different course of action, more ambitious than limiting himself to attacking Acapulco. Undiscouraged by Hidalgo's defeat, Morelos, on May 2, presented his officers with a plan to conquer most of southern Mexico as prelude to attacking the capital itself. The cause of independence had found a new leader. Though he lacked Hidalgo's intellectual brilliance, Morelos was to demonstrate superiority in military leadership and statesmanship.

The curate of Carácuaro was extremely fortunate in gathering about him a group of competent and brave officers. Hermenegildo Galeana was a rich cotton farmer, grandson of an English buccaneer who had settled in Mexico. Nicolás Bravo, a wealthy Creole hacendado who resisted appeals to join the royalist cause, had fled from the gachupines to hide in caves for several months, and in May responded favorably to Morelos' suggestion that he join the revolutionary cause. His four brothers served as well. Vicente Guerrero, a poor peasant, was to become commander in chief after Morelos' death in 1815. A priest from a small village, Mariano Matamoros, was considered the most capable military leader next to Morelos and served him as second in command. Manuel Félix Fernández became known by the pseudonym Guadalupe Victoria (for the Virgin and for Victory). There was even a North American—Peter Ellis Bean, a soldier of fortune who had been captured during a filibustering expedition in Texas in 1800 and escaped from the Spaniards ten years later to join Morelos at Acapulco. Valerio Trujano, a very brave mulatto, served Morelos also. Bravo, Guerrero, and Guadalupe Victoria, after serving the revolutionary forces with distinction, were destined to play prominent roles after the achievement of independence. Bean was sent in 1814 as envoy to the United States. The others were killed in the course of Morelos' campaigns.

From May until late that summer, Morelos marched and fought from Acapulco in the south to Cuautla, winning village after village, destroying or capturing royalist garrisons, and gaining new recruits. After setting up temporary headquarters in Cuautla, Morelos proceeded to raid the surrounding area, capturing Tenancingo and the great silver town of Taxco, finally returning to Cuautla in February, 1812.

⌒

Cuautla is located forty miles from Mexico City, well on the other side of the mountains that ring the Valley of Mexico. Viceroy Venegas had cause for worry; Morelos' unbroken string of victories heralded a formidable foe, much more dangerous than Hidalgo. The viceroy ordered Calleja to attack Cuautla with a sizable force of veterans.

Cuautla lent itself admirably to a strong defense. The town is located on a small hill, surrounded by rolling plains, so that the enemy had to attack from terrain that afforded little concealment and no natural protection. Morelos, committed to a resolute defense, commandeered every inhabitant—men, women and even children—to help in digging trenches and in adding to the fortifications.

An overconfident Calleja attacked Cuautla on February 19. Although his forces outnumbered the insurgents and were better equipped, the royalists were beaten back after repeated charges. The grim determination, courage, high morale, and clever tactics of the defense compelled Calleja to adopt siege tactics and to call for additional men and munitions. By early March, Calleja's forces numbered twice that of the 4,500 beleaguered insurgents who valiantly defended Cuautla against artillery bombardments, infantry, and cavalry attacks. The defendants' heroism was so extraordinary that Calleja acknowledged his admiration in a report dated April 24:

> If the constancy and activity of the defenders of Cuautla were in behalf of morality and directed to a just cause, they would merit some day a distinguished place in history. Hemmed in by our troops and harassed by necessity, they yet manifest joy in every undertaking. . . . This priest [Morelos] is a second Mohamet . . .*

Morelos and his men, however, could not withstand additional enemies almost as deadly as bullets and shells. Thirst and starvation, which had the inhabitants eating lizards, rats, and cats, were major allies of Calleja. Finally the resourceful Morelos led his army and some of the citizens out of the town one night in a brilliantly executed maneuver that caught Calleja by surprise. After almost seventy-two days of siege, the exasperated Calleja had won an empty victory. The royalists slaughtered men, women, and children who had remained in Cuautla.

Morelos had to change his original plans for attacking the capital. A new plan to conquer all the south was adopted. For six months after the Cuautla defeat, Morelos swept through southern Mexico, recapturing territory that had been retaken by royalists during the long siege. But

* J. A. Caruso, *The Liberators of Mexico* (New York, 1954), p. 111.

the curate was unable to consolidate newly won positions; for example, Orizaba and Tehuacán fell to the insurgents, only to be reoccupied by royalists almost immediately after Morelos' forces departed. Morelos did not have enough men to garrison permanently the towns being liberated. Skillful maneuvers, crisscrossing the countryside, were sufficient to baffle the viceroy's troops and to avoid head-on clashes that would unnecessarily commit the main body of insurgents to major engagements. Morelos' tactics also enabled him to choose the time and place for battle and to win a number of minor victories.

Yet they were minor. Almost all of the year 1812 had passed without the revolutionary cause being able to claim a substantial victory. Finally, in November, Morelos led a force of five thousand well-trained men to a brilliant victory at Oaxaca, capital of the province of the same name. Besides reviving insurgent morale and buttressing Morelos' personal leadership, the revolutionists gained materially. The fertile region supplied the army with food and sizable quantities of money and jewelry were obtained. During the more than two months that Morelos occupied the region, his forces were trained and augmented with additional recruits. Much needed military equipment was also acquired.

The loss of Oaxaca was a serious blow to the royalists in still another way: Calleja's reputation was further damaged. He and the viceroy engaged in useless recriminations until Calleja finally retired to his hacienda.

᠆᠊᠍ᢙᠣ

Losing Calleja's inestimable services was but one of many ills descending upon Venegas. During the year 1812 a great deal had taken place in Spain, historic events that were to have profound effects upon the colonies. The acting government in Spain, the Central Junta, had called a constitutional convention that included representatives from the American colonies. The delegates of the convention represented a wide range of political opinions, but the majority were liberals who had imbibed deeply ideas of the French Revolution. The Constitution of 1812 that was finally adopted was the most liberal document in all Europe. It made Spain a constitutional monarchy and included the ideological apparatus of the French Revolution. Incorporated in it were the guarantees of the rights of man, freedom of the press, representative government modeled on the parliamentary form in England, separation of powers, and elective municipal offices. Catholicism was established as the only official religion, but the Inquisition was abolished. Spain's overseas possessions were given equal representation, although the American delegates had demanded, unsuccessfully, provisions for self-government that would have made the Americas virtually independent.

In New Spain, Viceroy Venegas reluctantly published the new constitution on September 28. The article providing for freedom of the press brought joy to the liberals and dismay to the gachupines. An illegal press had been operating from the very beginning of the Revolution. The Society of the Guadalupes, a secret group in Mexico City, had performed many services for the insurgent army. They supplied Morelos with information, arms, money, and had been clandestinely publishing pamphlets and supplying the insurgent press with paper and ink. Next to arms and food, perhaps nothing is more important to a modern revolutionary movement than the existence of a press by which it can disseminate its ideas. Nevertheless, the newly established freedom of press proved an illusion, for Venegas simply ordered the arrest of those pamphleteers and other writers who were foolish enough to come out into the open.

One of the provisions of the new constitution called for election of municipal officers. The insurgents in Mexico City hoped to capture control of the cabildo, but their expectations were soon ended. When Venegas learned that all twenty-five electors were Creoles, he autocratically decreed that the old cabildo would remain in session.

Morelos was now convinced that he could never rely upon any peninsulars, at home or abroad. Only complete independence from Spain could satisfy the aspirations of Mexicans. All pretense of fighting in the name of Ferdinand VII must be cast aside, nor could any reliance be placed upon the liberal constitution of 1812.

In March of 1813 Calleja came out of retirement; the junta in Spain had appointed him as the new viceroy to replace Venegas. Carlos María Bustamante, member of the Guadalupes and an historian, characterized Calleja as "the new Tamerlane," a brutal, egoistical opportunist. The Guadalupes in Mexico City sent messengers to urge Morelos to attack the capital, but the priest did not consider the time propitious. Instead he resolved to fulfill Hidalgo's original commission to capture Acapulco. The port could be an important avenue of supply and communication, especially with nations whose support Morelos hoped to enlist.

Morelos left Oaxaca and marched overland to undertake a new siege of the busy Pacific port in April. Yet it was not until August 19 that the royalists finally surrendered. It is questionable whether Morelos had been wise in besieging Acapulco when he might have better employed his troops in more decisive campaigns in the heart of Mexico. The capture of the port city did not prove to be as important as Morelos had hoped.

Nevertheless the military success yielded a political victory for Morelos. The Guadalupes and other insurgent leaders had differed with Morelos on military and political matters. Now Morelos became the undisputed leader of the revolutionary government. At his insistence, a Congress was convened in Chilpancingo commencing September 14. The representatives were chosen in each provincial capital by plurality votes of delegates from every parish.

The Congress elected Morelos Generalíssimo, in addition to the modest title he had previously assumed as "Servant of the Nation." A constitution, formulated principally by Morelos, was drafted, but it was not proclaimed until later the following year. A representative republican form of government was established, and its first decrees embodied many of the social reforms previously enunciated by Morelos. A formal declaration of independence, written by the historian Carlos María Bustamante, was published in November. A slim foundation had been laid for the independent Mexico yet to be established. The program for social reforms was still only an expression on paper of ideals that were a long way from being realized.

Morelos resolved to consolidate his position in the south, but from this time on he was to suffer one defeat after another. An attempt to capture his birthplace, Valladolid, ended in disaster. During the next months the insurgents lost two of their best commanders, Matamoros and Galeana; Morelos in despair cried out that he had lost his right and left arms. For months Morelos lived in the jungles of Michoacán, finally emerging to take refuge in the caves of Atijo, near his old curate of Carácuaro. Royalist control, meanwhile, was being reestablished throughout the area that had been won at such cost.

Calleja determined to rid the country of the insurgent troops. Every available man was ordered into the field. Region after region was regained with relative ease. Oaxaca and Acapulco, two major prizes, were recaptured. Yet despite resounding royalist successes, they were unable to come to grips with the main body of the insurgents. The Congress and Morelos himself remained beyond their grasp. More than a year was to pass before the viceroy could satisfy his ambition.

The Congress led a nomadic existence, moving from one locality to another. At Uruapán, a fateful decision was made to remove some two hundred miles eastward to Tehuacán. Morelos, who had democratically subordinated himself to the Congress, was given the difficult assignment of escorting the representatives on their dangerous journey, which was to take them through royalist-held territory. For more than a month the Congress and its military escort of about one thousand men made their tortuous way east.

Apprised of the general movement of the insurgents, Calleja dispatched several detachments to deploy in areas through which the insurgents might be marching. One such detachment of six hundred men, under the command of Colonel Manuel de la Concha, did succeed in coming quite suddenly upon the convoy at Tesmalca, where the insurgents were resting after weeks of forced marching. A brief battle put an end to the insurgents' resistance. Most of the Congress were able to escape, owing to Morelos' self-sacrificing rearguard action; the Servant of the Nation and a number of other leaders were captured. The second phase of the Revolution had come to an end as tragic and as destructive as the first.

For three days Morelos was tried by the Inquisition, which found him guilty on twenty-six charges. The defendant was declared "a heretic, apostate of the holy faith, an atheist, materialist, deist, libertine, implacable enemy of Christianity and the state, a vile seducer, hypocrite, and traitor." The distinguished historian of the Inquisition, Henry Charles Lea, describes the trial as "the most expeditious . . . in the annals of the Holy Office—a grim comedy to gratify the vanity of the actors." On November 27, an auto-da-fé was held, in the course of which several hundred prominent people witnessed the act of defrocking Morelos.

Then came three days of trial by the State, which ended with the expected verdict of guilty and the pronouncement of the death sentence. On December 22 the blindfolded prisoner was made to kneel; after uttering his final prayers, two volleys in the back ended the poor curate's life. Mexico honors him today as *Benemérito de la Patria* (Well-deserving of the Country).

For the next five years, 1815 to 1820, the Revolution took on new aspects. The revolutionary forces were scattered; there was no revolutionary government; there was no single leader. The fires lit by Hidalgo and Morelos, however, were not completely extinguished. All Mexico was seething with guerrilla bands carrying out intermittent local warfare that kept most of the thirty thousand royalist forces busy. There were dozens of insurgent chiefs, heading bands that numbered from just a handful to large detachments of two thousand or more. The two outstanding guerrilla chieftains were Vicente Guerrero and Guadalupe Victoria, both of whom had fought with distinction under Morelos. Victoria conducted operations in the province of Vera Cruz, while Guerrero was active in the Mixteca wilderness, in the mountains near Acapulco, where he exacted a heavy toll in harassing maneuvers.

In 1817, with the appearance of Francisco Javier Mina, the revolution momentarily took on new life. Mina had been an intrepid guerrilla fighter in Spain during the war against Napoleon. He had been captured in 1811 but after Napoleon's defeat he was released and returned to Spain, where Ferdinand VII had assumed the throne. Ferdinand had promised to uphold the liberal constitution of 1812, but no sooner had he been crowned than he abjured the constitution and inaugurated a new tyranny. Mina soon got into trouble with the monarch. He went into voluntary exile, taking residence in London. There he became acquainted with the American general Winfield Scott, who related to him the stirring events of New Spain, including the tragic end that had befallen Hidalgo and Morelos. Mina's mind filled with ideas of revenge against Ferdinand and with romantic notions of adventure. He proposed a plan to several wealthy Englishmen who consequently financed an expedition led by Mina, assisted by a dozen volunteers of different nationalities. They sailed to the United States preparatory to invading New Spain.

From Galveston in the Spanish province of Texas, after having recruited a number of Mexicans and a few American adventurers, Mina sailed for Soto la Marina in the spring of 1817. From Soto he fought his way into the interior, up into the Sierra Madre, hoping to join up with other insurgents. Mina soon earned a reputation for boldness through a number of minor victories. These and his magnetic leadership attracted hundreds of followers. The threat posed by Mina's success alarmed the viceregal authorities, who sent out a punitive expedition that quickly put an end to the adventurer's meteoric rise. He was captured and suffered the same fate as the other heroes of the Independence; on November 11, 1817, he was executed by a volley of bullets in the back.

From 1817 to 1820 reaction seemed to be in the ascendant. In Spain, Ferdinand was consolidating an autocratic rule against which the liberals were unable to mount any effective resistance. In New Spain, the Revolution was limited to scattered guerrilla resistance mostly confined to south of the Valley of Mexico. Only Guerrero and Victoria continued to harass royalist garrisons, plundering, capturing silver convoys, and conducting sporadic raids. Ferdinand determined to rid New Spain of the troublesome guerrillas (and those elsewhere in the Americas) once and for all. During the last quarter of 1819, crack troops were assembled at the port of Cádiz from which several fleets were to sail to the Americas.

A number of naval and military officers were quite unhappy about the proposed venture. A conspiracy, led by Colonel Rafael del Riego, came to a head January 1, 1820. The Constitution of 1812 was proclaimed again, the revolt spread, and Ferdinand was forced to readopt, temporarily, the constitution that so limited his authority and that contained so many liberal provisions. The liberals in New Spain, when they learned the news, rejoiced that a new order was imminent.

The conservatives, however, reacted to the news in a completely unexpected fashion. The aristocrats, the upper clergy, wealthy Creoles, the gachupines now gave favorable consideration to the idea of independence! To them, the idea of living under the Constitution of 1812 was anathema. On the contrary, it would be better if they could remain in power, ruling in the old way in an independent Mexico and without instituting any of the revolutionary reforms that had been proposed by Hidalgo and Morelos or even those contained in the Spanish constitution. A fantastic plot was concocted by a group of highly placed conservatives who put their confidence in an energetic and highly ambitious royalist officer, Agustín de Iturbide.

♈

Iturbide had been a competent, resourceful, and brave officer fighting against the Revolution from its inception.

He had been Trujillo's adjutant at Las Cruces; he had participated in the relentless pursuit of Morelos; he was a veteran of many skirmishes and battles. Next to Calleja he was deemed Mexico's most capable royalist officer.

It is not known whether Viceroy Apodoca, Calleja's successor since 1816, was privy to the plot; he was persuaded to give to Iturbide command of royalist forces in the south with instructions to capture or kill Guerrero and Victoria. With the appointment of Iturbide, the conspirators' plan was ready to be put into action.

What Iturbide intended to do was to win over the rebels by force or by cajolery to unite in a campaign against the viceroy. Failing to defeat the insurgents in the field, Iturbide resorted to the second alternative. He sent a friendly letter to Guerrero proposing a truce and an interview to discuss plans for combining forces. The honest yet naive patriot was seduced by the program outlined by Iturbide. The program was contained in the Plan of Iguala, the first of many "plans" with which *caudillos* initiated antigovernment actions for the next ninety years in turbulent Mexico.

The Plan of Iguala set forth three principles, or the Three Guarantees: the first proclaimed the sovereignty and independence of the Mexican nation; the second confirmed that Roman Catholicism was the state religion and that no other would be tolerated; the third proclaimed the political and social equality of Europeans, Indians, Creoles, and the mixed castes. The Plan thus aimed at satisfying everyone: the liberal Creoles who dreamed of independence; the Indians and mestizos who were promised brotherhood; the Catholic clergy whose religion was to be guaranteed continued supremacy; the gachupines—the Europeans—whose fears of Creole ascendancy were laid to rest; and the military aristocracy, for the army was to be the vehicle for guaranteeing the three principles.

This was tempting bait for Guerrero, Bravo, and other insurgent leaders, and they accepted Iturbide's leadership. The northward progress of the Army of the Three Guarantees was marked by a succession of capitulations on the part of war-weary royalist forces. With very little bloodshed the independence movement surged to complete victory. Viceroy Apodoca was forced to resign. Juan O'Donojú, who had arrived in New Spain on July 31, 1821, as the last legally appointed representative of Spain, agreed to sign a treaty based more or less on the principles set forth in the Plan of Iguala. However, the treaty provided that an interim government would offer the crown of an independent Mexico, to be reorganized as a constitutional monarchy, to Ferdinand VII. If he should decline, the offer was to be made to several other princes as suggested alternates; if no European would accept, then a Mexican congress would elect a monarch.

An overjoyed Iturbide, clothed in a resplendent uniform, rode into Mexico City at the head of his troops on September 27, 1821. Proudly he acknowledged the populace's cheers of "Long live the liberator! Long live the Army of the Three Guarantees!" Mexico was independent at last!

⚬

All during the wars for independence, the Central American peoples were tenuously tied to the Spanish monarchy; ideas of independence were limited to a minority unable or unwilling to strike out for their beliefs. In 1820, however, the movement toward emancipation became quite strong. By September 1821 the Creoles were determined to free themselves completely from Spanish domination. Liberals wished to set up a republic. The majority chose to affiliate with the Empire of Mexico, established in May of 1822 with Iturbide crowned as Agustín I. Early in 1823, Agustín I was overthrown, the empire ended, and so did the Central American affiliation.

The vexing problem that remained was one that divided the leaders of Central America. They sharply disagreed over the question of forming one republic or dividing the region into several nations. Guatemala, overcoming decentralization tendencies, managed to assert her supremacy in a weak Confederation of Central America formed in 1824. But those wanting separation of the provinces continued their activities. Local caudillos seeking to achieve individual control were responsible for years of civil war and turmoil. In 1838 Nicaragua seceded from the union, followed by Costa Rica and Honduras late that same year. In February of 1839, the remaining two states, Guatemala and El Salvador, separated, putting an end to the experiment, although the dream of confederation persisted for many decades, well into the twentieth century.

౼౿

Independence! One might hear the sardonic laughter of the ancient Indian gods echoing from the mountaintops. The independence of Mexico and the five Central American nations did not mean the emancipation of the peoples.

Release from the burdens of imperial Spanish rule did not produce freedom for Indians and Negroes. Negro slavery had yet to be abolished; the change in government did not change the relationship between master and slave. Nor had the change in government affected the status of the Indian. Those who did not suffer the indignities of peonage lived in the mountains and in the jungles, isolated and ignored. The popular uprising led by Hidalgo and Morelos had been aborted. The emancipation of the Indian lay far in the future.

The status of the Church remained fundamentally the same; if anything, its power and wealth increased. The hierarchy opposed secular education and any institution or reform that would have lifted the Indians out of their poverty and ignorance.

The new chief power was the army, upon whose support the government and the Church rested. The disreputable character of the army and its strangulating influence upon political, social, and economic affairs arose out of its role in the many years of fighting in the war for independence. In the eighteen military districts the army commanders became local caudillos—despotic, corrupt lords inspiring terror and contributing to corruption and decay in their respective domains. An interminable succession of caudillos, local and national, continually jockeying for power, plagued the unhappy people of an unhappy land. Independence did not mean the restoration of peace and order. For more than fifty years Mexico was to be convulsed with civil war, anarchy, and revolution.

CHAPTER FOUR

The Revolution in La Plata

IN THE SOUTH AMERICAN CONTINENT THE movements for independence developed separately in the viceroyalty of La Plata, in the captaincy-general of Chile, and in the viceroyalty of New Granada. Each had its leaders, each its special problems, and each developed its own momentum. Besides having a common enemy, however, there was some degree of unity to the several revolutions. Argentinians aided Chileans to liberate their country. Both, along with Venezuelans, Colombians, and Ecuadorians, participated in the liberation of Peru. The fate of all the South American nations ultimately hinged upon the expulsion of the royalists in Peru, which remained the principal Spanish bulwark until the end.

But each region has its own history, which will be related to the whole at the appropriate time. We begin with the independence movement in the La Plata territory.

✌ LA PLATA

La Plata's seven provinces had been established as a vice-royalty in 1776, a step taken in recognition of their growing economic importance. The mines of Upper Peru (now Bolivia), once fabulously productive, were still a considerable source of wealth to the Crown. There was also the lucrative cattle industry, principally in the region of Buenos Aires. Hides, tallow, and other cattle products poured in an endless stream to Spain and to mining areas in the colonies. Another paramount reason for granting viceregal status to the subcontinent was the need for more direct military as well as political supervision to meet Brazilian attempts to encroach upon La Platine territory, most particularly in the Banda Oriental (now Uruguay). In addition, Spain had to keep watch against England, her traditional rival, whose maritime power in the South Atlantic posed a persistent threat.

The territory's population in 1810 was approximately three million, of which about half were Indians and close to half were mestizos; there were perhaps one hundred thousand Negroes and mulattoes, while the whites—Creole and peninsular—were a small fraction of the total. The upper class, peninsulars and the wealthier Creoles, were *estancieros* (cattlemen, owners of the large estates called *estancias*), merchants, clergy, professionals, and large farmers in the cultivated river valleys of the Río de la Plata in Paraguay and in the fertile western reaches of Argentina.

Tenant farmers—mostly mestizo and Indian—performed the agricultural labor on the land of the estancieros. The gauchos—Creole, Indian, Negro, and the admixtures—were in economic transition from wild, fierce, independent nomads of the pampas to cowboys working for wages on the huge ranches in the provinces of Buenos Aires, Entre Ríos, Santa Fé, Córdoba, and the Banda Oriental.

The city of Buenos Aires was the capital of the viceroyalty, the site of the royal audiencia and a bustling port through which poured a two-way traffic of merchandise: exports of hides, tallow, woods, wool, tobacco and *yerba maté* (Paraguayan tea); imports of manufactured goods.

During the last decades of the eighteenth century the Spanish throne had yielded to some of the demands of the leading citizens. A royal decree in 1778, only two years after the establishment of the viceroyalty, authorized direct trade between Buenos Aires and ports in Spain, and legalized intra-American trade between that port and other Spanish American ports. The consequent growth of trade stimulated the desire of the *porteños* (the citizens of Buenos Aires) and of the estancieros for complete freedom from trade restrictions. This desire was immeasurably heightened after freedom of trade was actually practiced as a result of the temporary seizure of Buenos Aires by the British in 1806.

England, long covetous of Spain's possessions in the New World, attempted to take every advantage of Creole dissatisfaction and Spanish weakness. In 1806 Spain was still an ally of Napoleon, Great Britain's bitter enemy; attempts to disrupt Spanish overseas commerce were perfectly in consonance with England's strategy. An opportunity presented itself after one of England's fleets had participated in the successful displacement of the Dutch colony at the Cape of Good Hope, at the tip of South Africa. Sir Home Popham, commanding a small fleet of warships and transports, sailed from the Cape to Buenos Aires. On June 15, 1806, a force of 1,500 men led by General William Carr Beresford landed on the coast and proceeded to invade the city of Buenos Aires.

At the moment of the British landing, Viceroy Sobremonte was in attendance at the theater. Informed of the danger, he fled precipitously, thereby inspiring a satirical couplet:

Al primer cañonazo—de los valientes—
disparó Sobremonte—con los parientes.

[At the first cannon shot—from the brave fellows—
Sobremonte shot off—with his relatives.]

This cowardly action did much to damage the already tarnished reputation of the Spanish monarchy and its bureaucracy. The humiliation was the more aggravating when the porteños saw how small a body of men had been able to take the city without firing a shot.

Beresford sent to London booty valued at $1,500,000. At the very moment that Beresford was being lauded and his unauthorized achievement hailed as a British victory, he was being defeated by a volunteer force of patriots organized and led by an Hispanicized Frenchman, San-

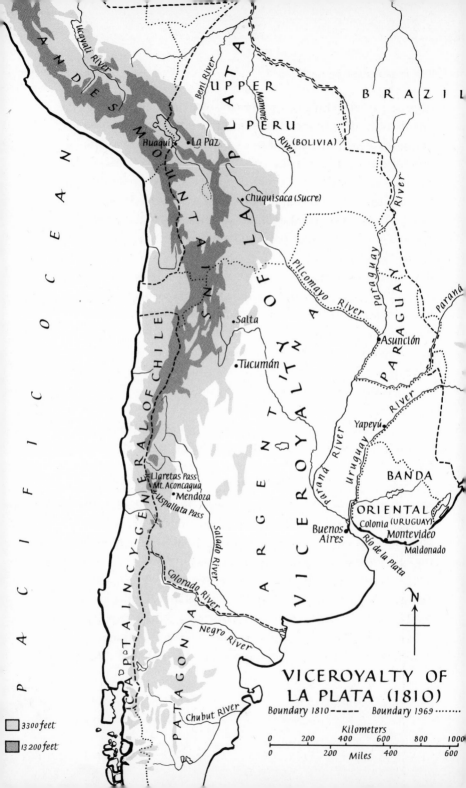

P A C I F I C   O C E A N

A N D E S   M O U N T A I N S

Ucayali River

Beni River

Mamoré River

U P P E R   P L A T A

P E R U

(BOLIVIA)

B R A Z I L

Huaqui
• La Paz

• Chuquisaca (Sucre)

Paraguay River

Pilcomayo River

• Salta

• Tucumán

Asunción •

P A R A G U A Y

Paraná

Paraná River

Uruguay River

Yapeyú •

C A P T A I N C Y - G E N E R A L   O F   C H I L E

Llaretas Pass
Mt. Aconcagua
Uspallata Pass
• Mendoza

A R G E N T I N A

Salado River

V I C E R O Y A L T Y   O F   L A   P L A T A

B A N D A
O R I E N T A L

Colonia (URUGUAY)
Buenos Aires •
Montevideo
Maldonado

Río de la Plata

Colorado River

Negro River

P A T A G O N I A

C A P T A I N C Y - G E N E R A L   O F   C H I L E

Chubut River

N

VICEROYALTY OF
LA PLATA (1810)

Boundary 1810 ----   Boundary 1969 ········

3300 feet
13 200 feet

Kilometers
0   200   400   600   800   1000

Miles
0   200   400   600

tiago de Liniers. On August 12, 1806, Beresford surrendered unconditionally. But the British fleet remained offshore, blockading both Buenos Aires and its sister port across the estuary, Montevideo.

Reinforcements were sent to the British, who assembled, by the beginning of 1807, an army of twelve thousand, a fleet of eighteen war vessels and more than eighty transports. The British were now committed to a major undertaking, part of a grand strategy to control Spanish possessions in the La Plata estuary and in distant Chile.

Ignoring the already discredited viceroy, the porteños took matters into their own hands. The cabildo, consisting of one hundred of the town's notables, met in open session; four thousand interested onlookers were prepared to intervene in the discussions if necessary. Liniers was placed in command of the military, the viceroy being peremptorily informed of a decision he dared not negate. This action of the cabildo, distributing civil and military authority, foreshadowed the future. The will of the Creoles was to become more and more decisive while the delegated authority of the Spanish Crown, as represented by the viceroy and the audiencia, steadily weakened in the next four years.

After successfully occupying Montevideo, Maldonado, and Colonia, the British marched on Buenos Aires. Awaiting them was a civilian militia of eight thousand, of which five thousand were Creoles; even the city's inhabitants assisted the militia in a spirited defense that stunned the invaders. Street barricades were thrown up at key intersections and the rooftops concealed some patriots, a few armed with rifles and others ready to hurl stones and all manner of crude missiles. The British veterans were deployed formally and unable to cope with the ferocity of carefully planned street-to-street and house-to-house combat, which they probably had never encountered before. The battle began early in the morning of July 5. By the end of the day the British had lost 1,130 killed and wounded, and about 1,500 were taken prisoner; whereas the American casualties were 302 killed and 514 wounded. The following day, General Whitelocke, the British commander, signed a treaty of capitulation and agreed to withdraw all his forces completely. The porteños had won an astounding victory that merited the congratulations they received from all over the South American continent.

The military victory, however, turned out to be the least significant aspect of the whole affair. Spanish law had been flouted with the creation of a wartime junta that ruled instead of the viceroy. The porteños had learned that they could not count on imperial aid and had proven that they were capable of defending themselves against a first-rate adversary. An additional taste, a most pleasant one, of the way economic affairs might be organized was the freedom of trade which the porteños and the Creoles of Montevideo enjoyed during the brief British occupation. The Creoles had long resented imperial restrictions that banned commerce with foreign powers. Although illegal trade had persisted, it could not be equated with the freedom the British had permitted for almost a year. That experience gave added impetus to the desire for independence, which had been slowly gathering momentum.

Members of the Lautaro Lodge, a secret society organized somewhat like a Freemason lodge, had been promoting ideas of independence. Creole nationalism had been stirred especially through the medium of newspapers published in Buenos Aires. Following the British invasions of 1806–7 and the Napoleonic invasion of Spain in 1808, agitation for independence grew more rapidly. Mariano Moreno, Creole lawyer and member of the cabildo abierto, composed a brief defending the economic interests of the estancieros and attacking the restrictive Spanish Navigation Acts. Manuel Belgrano, a wealthy Creole, secretary of the *consulado* (merchant guild) of Buenos Aires, was co-editor of the newspaper *Correo de Comercio*. In it he promoted the economic interests of Argentines and popularized the latest economic theories, such as Adam Smith's doctrines of free trade and laissez faire.

The tinder of revolution had been amassing for several decades before it was finally set afire.

౼

It has already been noted that the French invasion of Spain triggered the wars for independence throughout the Spanish colonies. When the news arrived that Charles IV had been compelled to abdicate and that the heir to the throne, Ferdinand VII, had been imprisoned by Napoleon, there was consternation and confusion. La Plata seethed with plots and intrigues. Montevideo set up a junta which refused to recognize the provisional viceroy, Santiago de Liniers (the patriot who had led the porteños against the British), who had been appointed by the audiencia in May of 1808. Simultaneously Martín Alzaga, an extremely wealthy Creole merchant, organized a plot in Buenos Aires. Liniers succeeded in quelling it but dissatisfaction with his regime increased. Liniers as head of the forces that defeated the British had been a hero. But now his French origin aroused distrust and he was unable to dispel rumors questioning his loyalty.

A *tumulto* (a popular uprising or mob action) on January 1, 1809, again challenged the viceroy's authority. The porteños demanded the establishment of a junta to replace all viceregal authorities. Liniers maneuvered a compromise which kept him in office, but he agreed to remove and exile the *regidores*—Spanish-appointed officials of the cabildo. One effect of this compromise was the growth of Creole sovereignty at the expense of viceregal authority. On the other hand, the viceroy was still powerful enough to resist the radical demand to institute a junta.

In May and July similar insurrectionary actions took place in two Bolivian areas—in the city of Chuquisaca and in the intendancy of La Paz. In the former, the envoy from the Central Junta in Spain was denied his office. In La Paz, a junta was created but the insurrection was forcibly crushed through the intervention of the Peruvian viceroy. In August the Central Junta in Spain replaced Liniers with Baltasar Hidalgo de Cisneros, but the colonists were not to be mollified. The patriots were no longer content with halfway measures or compromises: revolution was in the air.

The explosion came in May 1810, when Viceroy Cisneros announced that the Central Junta at Seville had been forced to flee from the French army. On May 20, the patriot members of the cabildo requested the viceroy to convoke a cabildo abierto immediately. Cisneros responded by summoning the military commanders to meet at the fortress that same evening, asking them to help him in maintaining order and to support their king and country. Some of the Spanish commanders pledged their loyalty, but the others equivocated.

At that very moment members of the Lautaro Lodge resolved to send a deputation at once to demand that the viceroy convoke a cabildo abierto. The two delegates, Juan J. Castelli and Martín Rodríguez, found the viceroy, whose fruitless meeting with the military had just concluded, playing cards. Castelli and Rodríguez informed the viceroy that he was no longer in authority and that the people duly assembled would deliberate his fate. Rodríguez bluntly stated that the delegation had but five minutes to return with the viceroy's reply. Cisneros very reluctantly acceded to the demand and announced his decision on the following day to the people assembled in the main plaza.

The cabildo abierto began its deliberations in the morning of May 22. The 251 present included 60 military officials; 39 civil employees; 25 members of the clergy; 26 professionals, mostly lawyers; and 94 merchants, landowners and other persons. Two principal alternatives were considered: retaining or deposing the viceroy. A majority of 155 voted for deposition. It was also decided that the cabildo should determine the form of government. But the cabildo, half of whose members were Spaniards, was more moderately disposed than the determined Creoles who dominated the cabildo abierto. On May 23 it adopted a compromise solution, which it put into effect the following day. The cabildo created a junta that was to rule instead of the viceroy and appointed Cisneros as its president. By stripping Cisneros of his viceregal powers yet retaining him in some official capacity, the moderates in the cabildo hoped to retain closer ties with Spain as well as to maintain their dominance over the porteños.

This compromise was not acceptable to the porteños, particularly to the more militant patriots of the secret society. That very evening, May 24, the society met and determined that it would resort to arms if necessary in order to carry out the "popular will." Two emissaries went to Cisneros, made known their desires, and forced his resignation.

On historic May 25, the cabildo convened once again while outside the hall a clamorous populace gathered to await its decision. There was no other recourse for the notables but to yield. A patriotic junta was established with Cornelio Saavedra as president and Mariano Moreno and Juan J. Paso as executive secretaries. These three were to be responsible to the cabildo abierto. Thus the Creoles had not only rejected the authority of Spain but had gone even further by defying the authority of the cabildo with its Spanish overtones.

The militancy of the porteños had prevented any conciliatory action. The creation of the junta in Buenos Aires was a revolutionary act that in effect established the independence of the La Plata region. Although the junta announced it was ruling in the name of the king, it soon became apparent that this was merely a subterfuge. The actual declaration of independence was not promulgated until July 9, 1816, but this was simply confirmation of what was an accomplished fact; May 25, 1810, is the date celebrated as the beginning of emancipation.

✌ PARAGUAY

The junta in Buenos Aires aspired to make their city the political and economic center of all the provinces that comprised the old viceroyalty. But sectional and local interests that had developed during the colonial period now challenged the sovereignty of the porteños. Paraguay, Uruguay, Upper Peru, and the interior provinces of Argentina proper all had economic concerns that conflicted with those of Buenos Aires and their political aspirations clashed with the porteños' dream of being the dominating center of a huge Argentine nation. With Spanish authority overthrown by the porteños, some of the provinces sought their own political independence. The way was open for civil war, anarchy, and caudillismo.

At the time of the revolution, Paraguay was the most densely populated of the La Plata provinces. Paraguay is an extremely fertile land with a benevolent climate. With its scenic beauty, it deserves its description as a physical paradise.

The Creoles who lived there had asserted a strong independent spirit in years of struggling against the secular power of the Jesuits, and in fighting the tax and trade policies of the Crown; they had long sought for an increased measure of local autonomy, most particularly in the capital, Asunción. Besides being anti-Spanish, the Paraguayans resented the porteños. Landlocked Paraguay depended for its economic intercourse upon the Paraná River which flows into the estuary controlled by Buenos Aires. The Paraguayan hacendados had no intention of subordinating themselves politically to the porteños.

Two months after Buenos Aires had taken its first steps towards independence, the Creoles in Asunción followed suit. Appeals from the junta in Buenos Aires that Asunción send delegates were rejected. The Paraguayans meant to move toward independence in their own way. General Belgrano appeared with an army in January 1811, in an effort to force Asunción to accept the leadership of Buenos Aires. The Creoles in Asunción hastily gathered a militia which very firmly and very successfully defeated the Argentine army.

The question of whether the new government of Paraguay should rule in the name of Ferdinand VII was very dramatically resolved in May. In the midst of the debate among the prominent citizens, Dr. José Gaspar Rodríguez de Francia placed a pair of loaded pistols upon a table and announced: "These are the arguments which I bring against the supremacy of Ferdinand VII." In June, Paraguay proclaimed its independence, and Francia was the first of a long line of dictators.

His despotic rule satisfied most Creoles and guaranteed continued misery for the Guaraní Indians.

✑ URUGUAY

Although the British occupation in 1807 of the Banda Oriental had been brief, its inhabitants were very much influenced by it toward independence. From the printing press contributed by the English emerged a weekly newspaper filled with anti-Napoleon diatribes and articles that contrasted England's democratic institutions with Spain's despotism. Freedom of trade, long desired by the Creoles, became a reality in the Banda Oriental as in Buenos Aires.

The Napoleonic invasion of Spain affected Orientales in much the same way as it had their brothers on the opposite side of the La Plata estuary. However, the Spanish garrison in the capital, Montevideo, was strong enough to prevent a Creole imitation of the Buenos Aires revolution of May 25. In 1811 the Buenos Aires junta sent an expedition to oust the royalist garrison in Montevideo. Simultaneously, in the interior, Orientales rose up against the Spaniards and enthusiastically supported the Argentines' siege of Montevideo.

The Spanish governor, Francisco Javier de Elío, appealed to the Portuguese in Brazil to come to his aid. And at about the same time, the royalists in Upper Peru posed a more serious threat to Buenos Aires. The Argentines decided to withdraw from the Banda Oriental temporarily in order to concentrate their efforts on invasions that might come from Upper Peru. Consequently they concluded an armistice with Elío, leaving the Orientales to their fate.

The Orientales were incensed at what they considered to be the selfish desertion of the porteños. The people responded to the daring leadership of José Gervasio Artigas, an intrepid Creole gaucho who had had considerable experience conducting guerrilla raids into Brazilian territory. Artigas, like Moses, led an exodus of thousands of men, women, and children; but unlike Moses, who led his people to their homeland, Artigas led his to exile. They crossed the Uruguay River to take refuge in what is now the Argentine province of Entre Ríos, so-called because it is situated between the Paraná and Uruguay rivers. They waited in the valley for fourteen long months before returning to their homeland when the armistice between the Buenos Aires government and Elío came to a sudden end.

Once again Montevideo was brought under siege by the porteños, ably seconded by Artigas and his hard-riding gauchos. But the ill feeling that had arisen earlier mounted when Buenos Aires refused to accede to Artigas' demand that the Banda be given autonomy. It was now the turn of the Orientales to withdraw from the siege, leaving the porteños to overcome the royalists. In January 1814 Artigas and his army encamped on the eastern shore of the Uruguay River. In June 1814 Elío finally capitulated to Buenos Aires, ending Spanish control in the Banda.

From 1814 to 1820 the Orientales were caught in a crossfire between Portuguese invaders and the Buenos Aires junta. In 1820, Brazil formally annexed the Banda Oriental.

During the next five years the Orientales plotted to liberate their country. In 1825, Juan Antonio Lavalleja led the armed struggle against Brazil. Buenos Aires hastened to the support of the Orientales, intending to annex the Banda once the Brazilians were defeated. Through the intervention of Great Britain peace was secured in 1828 between Argentina and Brazil and the independence of Uruguay was recognized by treaty. Set up as a buffer state between the two giant neighbors, the "Switzerland of South America" started off on the turbulent road of nationhood.

⌒

The period of national organization in La Plata from 1810 to 1825 was filled with internal disorders and sectional rivalries. The story of the disintegration of the viceroyalty into four independent entities, and in the early years, royalist attempts to recapture the La Plata territory, is best narrated as postindependence history although it is not completely divorced from the independence struggle. Royalist attempts to recover losses, however, are intertwined with the cause of independence in the rest of the continent.

Compared to the military problems faced by the revolutionaries elsewhere in the Spanish possessions, the emancipation movement in Buenos Aires had a relatively easy time. The La Plata provinces, with one principal exception, did not receive the attention that the royalists gave to the other revolutionary movements. The exception was Upper Peru, whose rich mineral wealth Spain was unwilling to part with so easily. Furthermore, from Upper Peru, royalist forces might easily penetrate the northern area of Argentina and at the same time be able to descend the rivers into Paraguay and thence to the La Plata estuary itself. Whether or not all the patriots in Buenos Aires were fully aware of it, the presence of strong royalist forces in Peru and Upper Peru made the preservation of their independence extremely doubtful.

In any case the patriots hoped to incorporate Upper Peru, part of the old viceroyalty, into the national framework. The junta sent an army of 1,150 soldiers to the interior provinces in the northwest that had risen against the Buenos Aires government. After quickly suppressing the uprising in Córdoba, the patriot army, under the command of Generals Balcarce and Castelli, moved north towards Upper Peru. A royalist detachment was overwhelmed, leaving the Argentines in temporary possession of the province. Royalist reinforcements from Peru routed the Argentines at the battle of Huaquí in July 1811, forcing them to retreat into Argentina. The disaster caused a crisis in Buenos Aires, leading to the dissolution of the junta and the formation of a triumvirate.

Spanish presence in Upper Peru was a powerful threat to the northern provinces of Argentina. From 1811 to 1815 patriot and royalist armies clashed several times, victory alternating with defeat. No battle was conclusive, for the Argentines could not drive the royalists out of Upper Peru and the royalists could not mount a strong enough offensive to invade and hold Argentine territory. By the end of 1815 the Argentines gave up hope of recovering Upper Peru, limiting themselves to a defense of the northern frontier of Argentina.

At the end of 1815 the independence movements throughout the Spanish possessions were on the wane, with the royalists in firm control everywhere except in La Plata.

In South America Peru was a royalist bastion, and Upper Peru was completely controlled by royalists. In the northern part of the continent and in Chile the emancipators hoped to revive the independence movements of their respective areas. La Plata, which had achieved independence, was torn with internal dissensions and fearful of invasion from Upper Peru. In 1815, in fact as early as April 1814, of the few men who clearly saw the danger, it was José Francisco de San Martín whose vision was most all-embracing as well as most daring. His was the grand strategy that was to assure the independence of not only La Plata but of all southern South America.

San Martín was born on February 25, 1778, in the Indian village of Yapeyú. At the time his father was the Spanish administrator of the Jesuit mission there; his mother, Gregorio Matorras de San Martín, was a Creole. In 1785 the family moved to Spain, where the father had been assigned to a military post in Málaga. Following the example of his father and his three older brothers, all of whom were soldiers, José chose a military career. He had considerable campaign experience fighting against the Moors, the French in 1793, and the Portuguese in 1801. While fighting the Napoleonic invaders he rose to the rank of lieutenant colonel of cavalry. In 1811 he was appointed commander of a regiment of dragoons.

Learning of the American revolutions, San Martín quite inexplicably decided to put himself at the disposal of the Argentine leaders. No evidence accounts for his determination to dedicate himself completely to the cause of emancipation—all that is known is that a British vessel brought him to Buenos Aires in March 1812.

San Martín joined the Lautaro Lodge, which had been at the center of the independence movement, but he wished to take an active role in military affairs. At first there was some suspicion of a man who for twenty years had been a soldier of Spain and who had lived there all his adult life. He was initially put in charge of training recruits. But soon he was involved in fighting and won signal honors. In December 1813 he replaced General Belgrano as commander of the army of the north defending the frontier against royalist incursions from Upper Peru.

San Martín became convinced that the Buenos Aires government's plan to liberate Upper Peru was not feasible. The royalists could and did get reinforcements from Peru. Peru, then, was the key. Nor was it militarily sound, reasoned San Martín, to invade Peru from Upper Peru even if the latter could be liberated. He conceived a grand strategy considerably different from that of the government. It would take longer, entail infinitely more sacrifice, and incorporate broad plans for the liberation of all the continent instead of the narrow nationalistic aspirations of the Argentines. To his friend Nicolás Rodríguez Peña, San Martín wrote a letter dated April 1814 in which he disclosed his as yet secret master plan:

A small well-disciplined army in Mendoza [a western Argentine city located in the foothills of the Andes, on the other side of which is the Chilean city of Santiago] to cross the Andes in order to exterminate the royalists in Chile. . . . Then, allying our forces, we shall go by sea to capture Lima. This is the road and not the other; you may be sure that the war will not be finished until we capture Lima.

To cross the Andes! That would be a more difficult undertaking than Napoleon's incredible passage over the Alps. To go by sea to Lima! In what ships? And how could the Spanish navy be swept away?

The first step in the execution of the grand plan was a modest one. Pleading poor health, San Martín asked to be relieved of his command at Tucumán. Then he secured the post of governor of the province of Cuyo. In the pleasant climate of Mendoza, the provincial capital, San Martín would train and drill recruits. At first he counted on coming to the aid of the revolutionary forces in Chile, which had been fighting since 1810. But that plan was disrupted when the Chileans suffered a major setback in October 1814, only two months after San Martín had arrived in Mendoza. In late October three thousand pitiful remnants of the Chilean patriot army straggled into Mendoza after retreating across the Andes by way of the Uspallata Pass.

Thus the future of Chilean independence became indissolubly connected with that of Argentina. San Martín's plans had to be considerably modified, and from October 1814 until January 1817 he devoted all his energies to preparing his Chilean campaign. At this juncture it is necessary to review the dramatic occurrences that had been taking place in the captaincy-general of Chile.

CHAPTER FIVE

Chile

IN THE COLONIAL EPOCH, THE LONG NARROW strip of territory known as Chile was part of the viceroyalty of Peru. At the time of the revolution Chile's borders extended from the forbidding slopes of Tierra del Fuego in the south to Coquimbo, about two hundred miles north of Valparaíso. On its eastern borders were the towering Andes, including Mount Aconcagua, 22,830 feet, the highest peak in the Western Hemisphere. In recognition of its economic importance Chile in 1778 was given the status of captaincy-general, a political subdivision that carried with it a considerable degree of autonomy.

On the *fundos*, or huge landed estates, in the Central Valley, wheat-growing and the cattle industry were two of the colony's three principal economic enterprises; the third was mining—gold, silver, and copper—in the north.

The colonial aristocracy, a landowning oligarchy, consisted of the peninsulars and the Creoles; a majority of the Creoles had some Indian ancestry owing to the high degree of miscegenation that prevailed from the earliest colonial days. Next on the social ladder were the mestizos, who constituted the overwhelming majority of the population. There were about twenty thousand Negroes (including mulattoes and zambos) out of a total population of five hundred thousand. By 1800 most of the Indians, and they were not many, were confined to the inhospitable area in the extreme south.

The conditions of the working class, never good in any of the Spanish colonies, were worst in Chile. The day laborers, called *rotos* (the broken, or ragged ones) and the tenant farmers, or *inquilinos*, barely eked out the most miserable short-lived existence. In contrast, the pampered upper class has been described as ostentatious, indolent, and the least educated of the several colonial aristocracies in the New World. The one university, San Felipe, founded in 1756, did not compare with the much older universities in the other Spanish colonies. At the time of the revolution there was not one printing press in all Chile. There was ample justification for calling Chile the land of contrasts: great beauty and fertility contrasted with arid regions and inhospitable climates; extreme wealth of the few and the abject poverty of the masses; an educated few and an ignorant majority.

❧

The outstanding Chilean hero of the revolutionary epoch was Bernardo O'Higgins, born on August 20, 1778, the illegitimate son of Ambrosio. The father was an adventurous Irishman who had emigrated to Spain, was entrusted with a post in Chile, became president of the captaincy-general and finally served as viceroy of Peru. He had neglected his son all his life, but he sought to make belated amends before he died in 1801. Bernardo, living a most penurious existence in Spain, was surprised to learn that his father, in his will, had bequeathed to him the bulk of an extremely rich estate.

As a young man, Bernardo had resided in England, 1794–99. There he came under the influence of the legendary Francisco de Miranda, a Venezuelan in exile who was particularly active in promoting Spanish American independence. It was through Miranda that the young Bernardo became enthusiastic about the possibility of liberating Chile. When he returned there in 1802, he functioned efficiently as manager of his father's estates, but politics were soon to dominate his life. Soon O'Higgins would put into practice the revolutionary principles he had absorbed from Miranda. He became acquainted with a few prominent citizens in whom he could place his confidence. Among them was Juan Martínez de Rozas, a brilliant, erudite lawyer who had been friendly with the Argentine patriots Belgrano and Castelli during his student days. It was Martínez de Rozas who was the true founder and patriarch of the Chilean revolution; San Martín and O'Higgins were to be the liberators.

つ

The revolutionary tendency had arisen out of the need for economic and political reforms that would further

Creole interests. From abroad, the American and French revolutions had an additional influence on some of the more enlightened reformers, notably Martínez de Rozas. Revolutionary sentiment was encouraged by the heroic resistance of the Argentine Creoles in repelling the British invasions of 1806–7. In the middle of 1808 the news of the French invasion of Spain struck the same responsive chord in Chilean Creoles as it had in all the Spanish colonies.

By 1809 two political tendencies were apparent. One group, led by enlightened Creoles, was moving in the direction of independence; the other, led by the high officials —mostly peninsulars—and conservative Creoles, was itself split among those who would support the French if they were to win and those who would be loyal only to a Spanish monarch. What held this second group together was their uncompromising opposition to independence.

Discontent was mounting, as was obvious even to the notoriously incompetent governor, Francisco Antonio García Carrasco. To meet the danger of insurrection, García Carrasco promulgated a variety of harsh and thoughtless measures. Conversation about the mother country was forbidden, and violators were persecuted to the point of imprisonment. He also ordered the expulsion of all foreigners, for he considered them dangerous propagandists. Arrests and imprisonments became common, especially after the news of uprisings in Quito and Chuquisaca.

Constantly on the lookout for conspiracy, García Carrasco finally stumbled upon one in May 1810. It had originated in 1808, when a group of patriots began to take some steps toward counteracting the governor's tyrannical

rule. Since there was no printing press, private correspondence among the leaders and occasional secret meetings were
the chief means of publicizing their views and of effecting
some kind of organization. The two principal centers of
revolutionary activity were Concepción, where Martínez
de Rozas was the leader, and Santiago, where José Antonio
Rojas was the foremost participant. Somehow the governor
learned of a secret meeting being held in the home of
Rojas. It was the night of May 25, 1810, the very day in
which the independence of Buenos Aires was effected,
when the house of Rojas was invaded by police agents.
They arrested three conspirators: Rojas, Juan Antonio de
Ovalle Silva, an official of the cabildo, and Bernardo Vera
Pintado, a highly respected Argentinian lawyer.

On the following day the announcement of the imprisonment of these three popular men aroused an immediate
protest. It became tumultuous when it was learned that
the patriots were to be exiled to stand trial in Lima, the
viceregal capital. The cabildo of Santiago, the merchants,
professional men, and even the audiencia appealed to the
governor to rescind his order of deportation. This he consented to do, though he held the three plotters for trial
in Valparaíso. This partial victory was the first major step
toward open rebellion.

It was not until the end of June that Chileans learned of
the success of the Buenos Aires rebellion on May 25.
Thoroughly frightened by the news and at a loss as to how
to proceed intelligently, Carrasco secretly decided to deport the unfortunate three after all. On July 10, a frigate
departed from Valparaíso with two of the prisoners aboard.

When the inhabitants of Santiago learned of the betrayal the next morning, the cabildo was immediately convoked without the required permission from the governor. The cabildo illegally authorized an open, enlarged session (cabildo abierto) in response to the angry crowds demanding entrance into the hall. Not knowing that the deportation order had already been carried out, the people were demanding that the governor once again rescind his order. Two days later, when the people learned that the frigate had already sailed, they took to arms. Armed patrols roamed the streets and there was open talk of removing the governor and establishing a junta. Such activity was not the conduct of reformers, but an open rebellion.

The royal audiencia temporarily forestalled the inevitable by compelling the resignation of García Carrasco, replacing him with the senile Conde de la Conquista, Mateo de Toro Zambrano. However, the more militant patriots were not content with halfway measures.

Activity and agitation increased rapidly. The ranks of the patriots swelled with militant young Creoles; they were the sons of the wealthy, officers of the local militia and a few officers of the regular army, professional men, and members of the lower clergy. The two principal centers of patriot organization were Santiago, where the cabildo provided the organizational focus, and Concepción, where Martínez de Rozas and O'Higgins became the leaders. The royal audiencia served as the nucleus of the opposition; its members were largely the hated peninsulars—the top civil, religious, and military officials.

With no printing press available, the patriots had to

resort to handwritten proclamations, revolutionary plac-
ards, and oral communication. One principal tract that
was widely read was the *Political Christian Catechism,* the
author of which has not been definitely ascertained. It was
an impressive catalogue of complaints against Spain and
the peninsular bureaucracy; it defended republican principles and called for the formation of a provisional junta
which in turn would arrange for the calling of a constitutional convention. Much of it is reminiscent of the Anglo-
American Declaration of Independence of 1776.

The peninsulars mounted a propaganda offensive of
their own. The clerical hierarchy appealed to the people to
be "constant, loyal, and faithful to their much-loved king
and lord." Reforms and revolutionary sentiments were
condemned as scandalous, treasonous, and opposed to the
will of God. It was pointed out that resistance to authority
was resistance to the orders of God. If the insurgents were
successful, the hierarchy warned, there would be no end
of disorder and of abominations—nuns would be violated,
pillage and murder would be commonplace. As elsewhere
in the colonies, the Church hierarchy unequivocally supported established authority, whereas many members of
the lower clergy actively supported the revolutionary
movements.

Fully aware of the power of royalist resistance, the
patriots did not rely solely upon agitation. Throughout
the countryside the people were being urged to be prepared
to take up arms; a network that might be likened to the
New England minutemen was organized, with young
Creole horsemen ready to carry messages into the rural
areas to arouse their countrymen.

The eighty-four-year-old governor felt overwhelmed and finally agreed to the patriots' demand to convene an extraordinary cabildo abierto. On the morning of September 18, the hall of the consulado was filled with "three hundred and fifty persons, with powdered hair, and ceremoniously dressed in frock coats, three-pointed hats, short pantaloons, silk stockings, shoes with silver and gold buckles, and wearing small swords." *

The governor tendered his resignation. The few Spaniards present were unable to speak against the noise of the assembled notables, who took up the chant, "We want a junta!"

There was no choice but to proceed to the business of nominating and electing nine people to constitute a governmental junta that would rule in the name of Ferdinand VII. As in the other Spanish colonies, ruling in the name of the imprisoned king became either a mask for, or a first step towards, virtual independence.

But great trials were yet to unfold and eight years of warfare were to take place before independence was a reality.

꠸

Among the first actions taken by the new government was to provide for defense. In addition to the presence of royalist garrisons and many royalist supporters in Chile, there was the very real, very dangerous threat of invasion from the Spanish stronghold in Peru. Economic reforms were instituted, most important of which was the establishment

* Luis Galdames, *A History of Chile*, trans. and ed. by I. J. Cox (Chapel Hill, 1941), p. 156.

of freedom of trade; manifestly there was a very close relationship between the political and economic interests of the Creoles. The governor was deported to Lima and the royal audiencia was dissolved; no vestige of Spanish governmental authority remained.

The idea of complete independence gained favor. A widely read tract, written by Father Camilio Henríquez, urged the formation of an independent republic. Following the political thinking of the American and French revolutions, the priest wrote: "Nature made us equal, and only by virtue of a free pact, made spontaneously and voluntarily, can another man exercise just, legitimate, and reasonable authority over us."

Meanwhile the nine-man junta in Santiago was a provisional government only, and it had yet to receive enthusiastic popular support throughout Chile. To widen its base and to form a representative government, the junta called for elections of deputies to a national congress. The first, and stormy, meeting of the congress was held on July 4, 1811.

The congress was divided into three major factions: reactionaries who desired the restoration of Spanish power; moderates who favored economic and political reforms but opposed complete independence; and the radicals, who desired complete severance of all ties with Spain. Among the most prominent leaders of the radical faction were Martínez de Rozas, Bernardo O'Higgins, Camilio Henríquez, Manuel de Salas, and Juan Antonio de Ovalle Silva (one of the two men who had earlier been deported). The reactionaries and the moderates constituted a majority of the congress, effectively obstructing solutions by the radicals.

Martínez de Rozas went south to Concepción, the other principal center of insurgency, to effect a coup to oust the reactionary deputies. In Santiago, impatient militant patriots turned to force to resolve the congressional impasse. José Miguel Carrera, a flamboyant, energetic, and thoroughly revolutionary Creole officer, led a military coup d'état. The reactionaries and conservative moderates in the congress were replaced with patriot deputies, the cabildo of Santiago was reorganized, and a new executive junta of five men was established. The Napoleonic tactics of Carrera were as extraordinarily effective as they were extralegal.

The new junta and the new congress were quickly recognized by most of the country. The life of the new congress was short, yet it accomplished much. Of the many political and social reforms, one stands out as a major lasting accomplishment: Chile was the first South American nation to abolish slavery. In retrospect, one might conclude that the new government might have led the Chilean people to democracy as well as to independence; but a combination of internal and external factors put an end to its great promise. An impatient and ambitious Carrera dissolved the congress in December 1811 and set up a dictatorship.

Under the military dictatorship a constitution was proclaimed in which the government was to be organized on republican principles. Nevertheless the curious fiction was still maintained that Ferdinand VII was the sovereign. A printing press was obtained through the beneficence

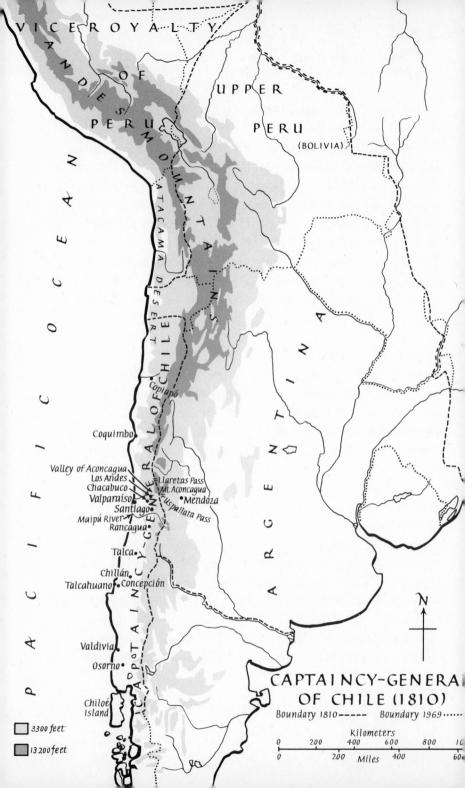

VICEROYALTY

ANDES

OF

PERU

UPPER

PERU

(BOLIVIA)

ATACAMA

MOUNTAINS

DESERT

CHILE

PACIFIC OCEAN

ARGENTINA

•Copiapó

Coquimbo•

CAPTAINCY-GENERAL OF

Valley of Aconcagua•
Los Andes•
Chacabuco•
Valparaíso•
Santiago•
Maipú River•
Rancagua•

Llaretas Pass
Mt. Aconcagua
•Mendoza
Uspallata Pass

Talca•

Chillán•
Talcahuano• •Concepción

Valdivia•

Osorno•

Chiloé
Island

N

CAPTAINCY-GENERAL
OF CHILE (1810)

Boundary 1810 ---- Boundary 1969 ······

☐ 3300 feet
▨ 13 200 feet

Kilometers
0   200   400   600   800   10[...]
0   200   400   60[...]
Miles

of a citizen of the United States, Mateo Arnaldo Hoevel, who was living in Santiago. A one-sheet newspaper, *The Dawn of Chile*, disseminated revolutionary ideas. In *The Dawn* appeared Chile's first national writers: Camilio Henríquez, a priest; Juan Egaña, a brilliant lawyer and author of the idea of a confederation of South American nations even before it was entertained by Simón Bolívar; Manuel de Salas, philanthropist and economist; and Manuel José Gandarillas, a young patriot.

A National Institute for the furtherance of secondary and higher education became a lasting achievement. There was much to credit to the Carrera dictatorship. On the other hand, it gave birth to intense discord that bordered on civil war. Martínez de Rozas, who was very much opposed to Carrera, was arrested, then exiled to Mendoza. O'Higgins' early dislike for Carrera developed into open hostility. Internal dissensions were threatening to tear the country apart when the long-expected invasion from Peru materialized early in 1813. The patriots temporarily put aside their disagreements and united to confront the enemy.

Peru's viceroy, Fernando Abascal, hoped to recover both the Platine provinces and Chile. One army was sent through Upper Peru to northern Argentina; simultaneously another went by sea to southern Chile, disembarking on the large island of Chiloé. It was militarily impractical to reach Chile from Peru by land, for it was necessary to cross the impassable Atacama Desert and then hundreds of miles of unpopulated wasteland. Chiloé, just off the coast and about one hundred miles south of Valdivia, remained pro-royalist all during the independence struggles, thereby affording an excellent base for military operations against the mainland.

To meet this peril, the patriots ended their private quarrels, named Carrera general-in-chief, and to support him, his two brothers, Juan José and Luís, and O'Higgins and his friend Juan Mackenna.

At the outset the Peruvian invasion of southern Chile was successful. Then followed a year of bitter but inconclusive fighting: the southern half of Chile, including the provinces of Concepción, Valdivia and Chiloé, remained royalist; Santiago and the north continued under patriot rule. In the course of the fighting O'Higgins displayed considerable military ability, whereas the Carrera brothers were sharply criticized by the junta. Not long afterward, two of of the brothers were captured by the royalists.

The devastation produced by the war induced both parties to seek peace; the Treaty of Lircay was signed in May 1814. One of its provisions stipulated the release of the Carrera brothers, but before it could be effected, the two prisoners escaped under mysterious circumstances. It was suspected that the Spanish commander had permitted the escape in the belief that the Carreras would contribute to internal disturbances, and the events that followed make the charge quite credible. In Santiago, the Carreras executed a military coup d'état and once again installed José Miguel as dictator.

One of Carrera's first actions was to deport individuals, including O'Higgins' friend Juan Mackenna, suspected of hostility to Carrera rule. O'Higgins refused to recognize the new leader, and civil war began. (Such fratricidal strife was common to many of the independence movements in the Spanish colonies. The cause that bound men together was not strong enough to prevent passion and disparate interests from erupting into violent conflict.)

One battle in this civil war had been fought and another was about to begin when the news arrived that the Treaty of Lircay had been repudiated by the viceroy in Peru. A fresh, large royalist army under the command of General Mariano Osorio had landed and moved on to Chillán. Osorio demanded the immediate surrender of all revolutionary forces. Carrera and O'Higgins once again resolved to bury their differences and agreed to unite the two armies. Carrera was to be the leader, but O'Higgins, commanding his own forces, was to constitute the vanguard, at his own request.

O'Higgins with seventeen hundred men took up a strong defensive position in the town of Rancagua. A few miles north, José Miguel Carrera with the main body of patriots awaited the call to action. Osorio marched up from the south with five thousand disciplined veterans and drafted Chileans. The battle of Rancagua began on October 1, 1814, and continued without letup into the following day. During the thirty hours of fierce fighting, Carrera never came to help the besieged forces of O'Higgins. O'Higgins and his men displayed the most extraordinary valor, but had to succumb to the superior forces of the enemy. Only five hundred men escaped. O'Higgins never forgave what he believed to be the cowardice and duplicity of José Miguel Carrera and his brother Luís.

The catastrophe at Rancagua signaled the end of the insurgent government. After Osorio triumphantly entered Santiago, he began to undo the four years' work of the patriots. Ferdinand VII had been back in power since May; Osorio was merely fulfilling his duty in applying with full vigor his sovereign's reactionary policy to the restored colonial regime in Chile. A new governor of Chile, Marcó del Pont, initiated a reign of terror worse than anything the Chileans had ever experienced before.

Seeking refuge in Argentina, O'Higgins, the Carrera brothers and three thousand patriots struggled painfully across the Andes until they reached Mendoza, where they were warmly welcomed by San Martín, who had assumed the post of governor of the province just two months earlier. His plan had been to lead an army of Argentines from Mendoza to aid the Chilean patriots to liberate that country as a first step toward the invasion of Peru. The disaster in Chile complicated matters considerably, but San Martín was not diverted from his original intentions. No South American nation could be assured of emancipation while the Spaniards held power in Peru. The best way to attack Peru, San Martín still firmly believed, would be by sea, using Chile as the base of operations.

꒰ᴖ꒱

San Martín was engaged in preparations for the great undertaking from October 1814 until January 1817. Recruiting, training, amassing munitions, constructing special equipment to make it possible to take artillery over the Andes, acquiring clothing, food, mules, horses, and obtaining funds were his constant preoccupation. Getting aid from the Buenos Aires government proved exceedingly difficult, for it was beset with a dozen thorny problems, many of which have already been discussed.

The populous and agriculturally rich Paraguay had split off from Buenos Aires and had formed its own independent government in 1811 under the dictatorship of Francia. Brazil had invaded Uruguay, where José Gervasio Artigas was leading his gauchos against both Brazilians and Argentines. Northern Argentina was under continual attack from royalists descending from Upper Peru. Sectional rivalries between the provinces in the interior and Buenos Aires presented grave political and economic problems. Buenos Aires' governments rose and fell; this instability added to an almost anarchic situation. This was the situation when San Martín in Mendoza was pleading for the necessary aid for an invasion of Chile.

Meanwhile, in Mendoza, the Carreras proved to be a disruptive influence from the day of their arrival. San Martín resolved the problem by having them sent off to Buenos Aires. There the rivalry between emigrant Carreristas and O'Higginists continued unabated. The authorities were thoroughly disgusted when Juan Mackenna was killed by Luís Carrera in a duel. From that moment the attempts of the Carreras to curry favor with the Argentine government were fruitless. José Miguel betook himself to the United States of America, hoping to secure aid.

In 1816 the internal dissensions in Argentina were partially allayed with the activities of a national congress, convened in Tucumán, which formed the United Provinces of

Miguel Hidalgo y Costilla

José María Morelos

Augustín de Iturbide

José Francisco de San Martín

Bernardo O'Higgins

Simón Bolívar

José Antonio Páez

Antonio José de Sucre

La Plata. It continued a directorate form of rule, appointing Juan Martín Pueyrredón, a close friend of San Martín's, as Supreme Director. Pueyrredón, in full agreement with his friend's plan to cross the Andes, hastened to give as much support as he could muster. On July 9, 1816, a formal declaration of independence was promulgated by the congress, thus climaxing what had already been a reality following the historic events of May 25, 1810. The declaration also had the immediate effect of buoying the spirits of the troops being trained in Mendoza.

From July to December the pace of preparations was feverish. Finally San Martín was ready to carry out his long-cherished dream. The army of five thousand departed from Mendoza on January 19. To deceive the enemy, San Martín divided the army into six unequal detachments to cross the Andes at five different passes; they were to divert and confuse the enemy. One of them, a moderate-sized detachment commanded by Juan Gregorio Las Heras, a Chilean veteran, was to cross by the Uspallata Pass, after which it was to join the bulk of the army. The main force was made up of two divisions, one commanded by O'Higgins and the other by San Martín himself. After crossing through the Llaretas Pass, this group was to join Las Heras' contingent in the Valley of Aconcagua and to march on Santiago or Valparaíso, depending upon the positions taken by the enemy. A sixth small group of about two hundred men crossed the Andes through another southern pass to create an additional diversion.

To confuse enemy intelligence further, San Martín resorted to yet another stratagem. He invited to a splendid feast and palaver the Tehuelche Indians, a warlike tribe that had remained aloof from Spaniards and Creoles alike. He bribed the Indians with gifts to secure a pledge that they would permit his army peaceful passage through their lands and asked them to serve as guides. The Indian chief was led to believe that a particular Andean pass was to be used by San Martín, whereas he was actually counting on the Indians to betray him. The information was forwarded to the Spaniards by the Indian chief, who thus obtained additional gifts. The Spaniards accepted the false information as true, and the route of San Martín's main force was protected from Spanish discovery.

⌒

Napoleon's crossing of the Alps at an altitude of 8,500 feet has been justly acclaimed as a prodigious feat. What then shall be said of San Martín's accomplishment of crossing the Andes at heights of from 12,000 to 15,000 feet, through terrain even more difficult than that encountered by Napoleon's troops? The men crossed in sight of the awesome snow-capped Mt. Aconcagua. They had to tramp through snow, along huge glaciers and above bottomless crevasses, their feet tortured by interminable miles of broken rocks and brittle volcanic ash, and from time to time they had to ford raging mountain torrents with icy waters that chilled the men to the bone. San Martín, writing in exile ten years later, noted:

The difficulties that had to be overcome in the crossing of the cordilleras can only be imagined by those who may have passed through them. . . . The chief problems were the lack of habitation and roads, the lack of game and above all the lack of pastures. The army had 10,600 saddle and pack mules, 1,600 horses and 700 head of cattle, and despite the most scrupulous care, only 4,300 mules and 511 horses in very bad condition reached Chile; the rest had died or were rendered useless in the mountains. . . . The *puna* or *soroche* [a mountain illness arising from the lack of oxygen] had affected the major part of the army, causing the death of several soldiers besides those who perished from the intense cold.*

The Spanish governor, Marcó del Pont, had 5,000 men at his disposal but he did not know how to deploy them to meet the several invading forces, so well had San Martín's strategy worked. The gorges seemed to be vomiting forth patriots from a dozen different places. By the time Del Pont realized he had been tricked, it was too late. He sent a force of about 1,500, commanded by General Rafael Maroto, to a ranch called Chacabuco near the village of Los Andes just outside the Valley of Aconcagua. A combination of superior force (San Martín had massed three thousand men at this spot), skillful tactics, the outstanding bravery of a battalion of Negro ex-slaves, and O'Higgins' heroism won the day. The Battle of Chacabuco, February 12, 1817, was a major turning point in the independence movement. The governor fled toward Valparaíso but was intercepted by a patriot detachment and captured. San Martín marched to Santiago, where he and his gallant men were warmly received.

The Creoles immediately proceeded to form a govern-

* Quoted in Ricardo Rojas, *El Santo de la Espada* (Buenos Aires, n.d.), p. 143. (My translation–A.P.)

ment. The cabildo offered San Martín the honor of heading the government, which he refused, urging instead that
O'Higgins be assigned the task. O'Higgins was appointed
Supreme Director and promptly went about instituting a
national government. In addition, he was concerned with
the formidable problem of dealing with powerful royalist
resistance in the south.

While the patriots were able to recapture Concepción,
they could not dislodge the Spaniards from their strong
defenses in the strategic port of Talcahuano. For months
the defenders withstood the vigorous siege, giving the
Peruvian viceroy, Pezuela, the time to equip and prepare
a new army. In January 1818 a force of 3,300 men commanded by General Osorio reached Talcahuano, relieving
the besieged Spaniards. With a portion of his fleet blockading the port of Valparaíso, Osorio and the bulk of his men
moved northward toward the capital.

The partial successes of O'Higgins to attain national
unity were being thwarted by Osorio's military threat. In
an effort to arouse his own troops as well as to draw the
country's support behind him, O'Higgins read to his men
the formal Declaration of Independence of Chile, February
12, 1818, coinciding with the first anniversary of the Battle
of Chacabuco. In all the cities and key towns controlled by
the patriots, the inhabitants swore an oath of allegiance to
the independent Chilean nation. O'Higgins expected this
action to promote a desperately needed national unity.

The Declaration of Independence partially produced
the desired result. Effective unity among most Creoles was
realized, although many still had to be forced to yield food,

clothing, supplies, and money to the patriots. But most of
the people were apathetic. It was still a matter of indifference to the peons, to the masses of serf-like peasants, whether
they were exploited by Spaniards or Creoles. The unity that
O'Higgins so urgently desired was hampered from the
outset since little consideration was given to the kind of
radical social reform that would be meaningful to the rotos
and inquilinos. The war was fundamentally a battle for
ascendancy between Creoles and Spaniards. The lower
classes, constituting the majority of the population, were
drawn into the conflict as they were drafted by whichever
force was nearest. Mestizo volunteers could be found fighting for the Creoles and for the Spaniards.

Leaving a thin defense around Valparaíso, San Martín
hurried to join O'Higgins south of Santiago to await the
attack of the royalists near Talca. On March 18, 1818, the
two armies clashed on the plains of Cancha Rayada, on
the outskirts of Talca. In less than half an hour the battle
was over, with disastrous consequences for the patriots.
O'Higgins was seriously wounded; many of the new recruits deserted; battalions retreated in panic. Fear spread
to Santiago, and all along the line of retreat inhabitants
were fleeing with their possessions.

The royalists crossed the River Maipú, just south of
Santiago. On the plain, within sight of the streets of the
city, the royalist army of five thousand engaged the patriot army of about equal size: Osorio versus San Martín.
From dawn on Sunday morning, April 5, until late afternoon a particularly bloody battle raged. Messengers
brought news periodically to the people still in Santiago,

including O'Higgins, whose wounded right arm had kept
him from the battle. Finally, despite his wound, he rode
to the battlefield, reaching the tent of San Martín at the
moment when the patriot victory was just about assured.
O'Higgins embraced San Martín with his left arm, exclaim-
ing: "Glory to the savior of Chile."

"General, Chile will never forget the name of the illustrious invalid who today presents himself in that state on
the field of battle," San Martín replied. Then both generals
galloped off to witness the last of the royalists being defeated at nearby Lo Espejo.

The patriot army had been defeated only fifteen days before, and many had thought that the cause was hopelessly
lost. But this time the patriots had won an outstanding and
complete victory. Out of the entire royalist army of five
thousand only two hundred men, including Osorio, escaped.
The decisive Battle of Maipú assured the independence of
Chile.

The old rivalry between the followers of O'Higgins and
the Carrera brothers was revived almost immediately after
the achievement of independence. José Miguel Carrera had
won the support of some adventurous North American
shipowners and merchants. They financed the equipping
of three ships with which José Miguel sailed to Buenos
Aires. He arrived just about the time that the Battle of
Chacabuco was about to be fought. Fearful that Carrera
might prove to be disruptive, Pueyrredón, the Supreme
Director, refused him permission to disembark; Carrera
fled to Montevideo for safety. Shortly thereafter he learned
that his two brothers had been executed in Mendoza—after

they had made a vain attempt to cross the Andes with the avowed aim of overthrowing the newly inaugurated O'Higgins. O'Higgins further antagonized Carrera supporters when he ordered the arrest of the very able guerrilla leader Manuel Rodríguez, who had fought bravely against the Spaniards from the very beginning. Rodríguez was shot under the most suspicious circumstances; it was alleged that he had tried to escape while he was being escorted out of Santiago to a place of banishment. These tragic events yielded even more tragic consequences, for the executions earned O'Higgins the animosity of the many Carrera supporters in Chile. The enmity was increased all the more in 1821 when José Miguel Carrera was imprisoned and executed in Mendoza. O'Higgins' dictatorship rested on a precarious base from the beginning.

The Battle of Maipú ended all serious royalist resistance in Chile, although some garrisons, notably in Chiloé, Valdivia, and Talcahuano, had still to be overcome. For Chile the war of independence was over. However for San Martín and all those who supported his grand strategy, the winning of Chile was only a stage preparatory to the winning of Peru.

CHAPTER SIX

San Martín
in Peru

To cross the land barriers between Chile and Peru was as impractical for San Martín looking northward as it had been for the royalists when they were aiming southward. Only by transporting troops via the sea could an effective military attack be launched against the viceregal capital, the principal royalist base in South America. But in April 1818 there was no Chilean navy!

Any hope San Martín might have entertained for the services of the Argentine navy were soon discarded. Buenos Aires was preoccupied with continuing internal dissension and very real external threats. So serious was the situation that at one point Buenos Aires ordered San Martín to return along with the volunteer Argentine troops still on Chilean soil. San Martín chose to disobey, thereby cutting himself off from any aid from Argentina and placing sole reliance upon the Chilean government to supply the resources—naval and military—to prosecute the war in Peru.

That O'Higgins determined to assume the responsibility of supporting his friend was an act of foresight and courage. He understood and therefore approved San Martín's plan; on the other hand, he had to deal with the multitude of internal problems, not the least of which was a growing antipathy of the war-weary Creoles to financing adventures abroad when so much was still needed at home. Nevertheless O'Higgins, in his capacity of Supreme Director, was able to convince Chileans that it was necessary to have a Chilean navy at least to protect Chilean ports and to attack those ports still in Spanish possession.

With funds from the Chilean treasury some foreign ships in the harbor of Valparaíso were purchased. Additional vessels were purchased from the United States and from England. Manuel Blanco Encalada, a young Spanish naval officer who had deserted to the patriot cause, became the first commander of the small navy. A scouting cruise in the vicinity of Talcahuano netted several Spanish ships that were immediately incorporated into the Chilean fleet. The energetic Blanco Encalada kept busy training sailors and marines.

Meanwhile a Chilean agent in London had been most fortunate in procuring the services of Lord Thomas Cochrane, who agreed to accept the direction of the Chilean navy. Cochrane had had a brilliant, though brief, career in the British navy, in the course of which he gained a reputation for great daring and resourcefulness. Cochrane arrived in Valparaíso in December 1818, and in January he set out on his first exploratory expedition, with Blanco Encalada serving as vice-admiral and William Miller, another Englishman, as commander of the marines.

Cochrane's four frigates reconnoitered the Peruvian coast, giving special attention to the strong defenses of Callao, the port serving Lima. Besides getting valuable information, Cochrane captured several Spanish prizes, and his intrepidity so frightened the enemy that they dared not venture forth from the security of the heavily fortified harbor in Callao.

In the Chilean coast, Cochrane executed a spectacular attack upon Valdivia, which had remained in royalist hands. Having freed that port, the whole of the Chilean coast, with the exception of Chiloé, was safely in Chilean hands. On the strength of such victories, Chile's prospects looked good to foreign investors, from whom it became easier to borrow money for financing the big expedition to Peru.

Two years of preparations produced an army of 4,200 to embark upon sixteen transports and eight war vessels, with their own complement of 1,800 sailors and marines. A little more than half the men were Chileans; the rest were Argentines. General San Martín was in command of the entire expedition, much to the chagrin of Admiral Cochrane, who would have liked to share the leadership; in fact, the colorful, tempestuous Englishman would have preferred to have been placed in sole command. The rivalry between the two men was bound to lead to difficulties. San Martín characterized Cochrane as "a great child who will give a lot of trouble, but his services may prove invaluable."

His observation turned out to be eminently correct on both counts.

As the great expedition sailed out of Valparaíso on August 20, 1820, O'Higgins was said to have remarked: "On those few timbers depends the fate of America."

Cochrane favored a direct attack upon Callao and Lima, upon the royalists in their strongest positions. San Martín proceeded much more cautiously and not solely for military reasons. He hoped to achieve the liberation of Peru with the aid of Peruvians. They would be encouraged, he hoped, to take matters into their own hands as soon as the presence of the liberating army would become known. To the Peruvians San Martín expected to distribute a proclamation written by O'Higgins in which he addressed them thus:

You shall be free and independent; you shall form your own government and your laws according to the spontaneous wishes of your own representatives. The soldiers of the army of liberation, your brothers, will exert no influence, military or civil, direct or indirect, in your social system. Whenever it suits you, dismiss the army which marches to protect you. A military force should never occupy the territory of a free people unless invited by its legitimate magistrates.

In O'Higgins' view the Peruvians were not free, therefore the army of liberation did not have to await an invitation. However, it is quite significant that both liberators were concerned only with helping to liberate, note to conquer, Peru.

The first landing was made at Pisco, about one hundred miles south of Lima, while Cochrane undertook to

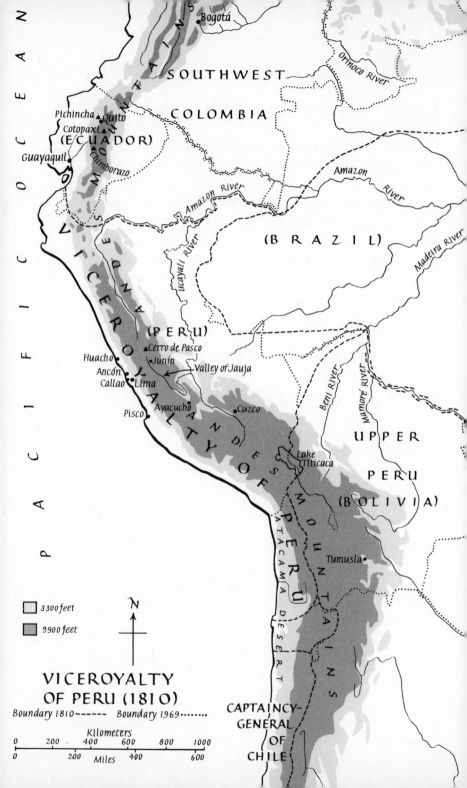

blockade Callao. There San Martín set up camp, but to his great disappointment, the inhabitants betook themselves, their possessions, and their Negro slaves into the interior. Peruvians were not quite as eager to assert their independence as San Martín had optimistically expected.

The new liberal government in Spain had sent instructions to Viceroy Pezuela to attempt to conciliate San Martín. From the end of September to October 4, talks between the viceroy's envoys and San Martín were to no avail; the viceroy could not accept conditions demanded by San Martín that would have meant the virtual independence of Peru and Upper Peru.

Immediately upon the conclusion of the negotiations, San Martín sent a reconnoitering force of 1,300 men commanded by Colonel Arenales into the interior. An initial successful encounter with royalists was dissipated when Arenales, under orders, returned to the coast. The Indians who had welcomed Arenales were slaughtered by the royalists. As was often the case, the Indians were unfortunate pawns in the conflict between Creoles and peninsulars.

In January 1821, San Martín left Pisco, sailed north, disembarked with his army at Huacho, and set up camp about seventy-five miles north of Lima, thus cutting off the viceroy's communications with the northern provinces and establishing a strategic base from which to capture Lima. Raiding expeditions sent into the interior brought back plunder—silver from the Cerro de Pasco mines. Cochrane, *El Diablo,* as he came to be called by the Spaniards, and Miller with his marines, harassed settlements all along the coast, while a portion of the fleet maintained a tight blockade of Callao.

Although not decisive victories, the successes of the liberators disturbed the Spanish officer caste; they deposed Pezuela and replaced him with General La Serna; General Canterac was appointed commander of the royalist armed forces. The new leaders decided to abandon Lima, withdrawing the main body to the mountains but leaving a strong garrison in Callao.

So it was that, in July, San Martín was able to enter Lima peacefully. Of all the major capitals of South America, Lima was exceptional in never having had a strong independence movement. Ideas of independence suddenly became popular with the presence of the liberating army. The cabildo met. A cabildo abierto was convened. It was the unanimous view of the notables that Peru should be declared independent. On July 28, 1821, the citizens assembled in the main square, swore allegiance to the new nation, and signed their names to the declaration of independence. Church bells rang, troops paraded, the people shouted their "Vivas!", the artillery boomed, and a new flag (designed by San Martín) was unfurled. Thus was independence declared, but its achievement was still a long way off.

Independence had been thrust upon Lima. Its citizens, unlike those in other Spanish capitals, had never broken with royal authority. The leading citizens were unprepared to assume power. The masses—mestizos, Indians, and Negroes—were not consulted. It would be incautious and imprudent, San Martín reasoned, to put power into their hands. In a proclamation addressed to the people, the liberator explained:

In the first place, liberty, which is the most ardent object of our wishes, must be bestowed with caution, in order that the sacrifices made for the purpose of gaining it be not rendered useless. Every civilized people is entitled to be free; but the degree of freedom which any country can enjoy, must bear an exact proportion to the measure of its civilization: if the first exceed the last, no power can save them from anarchy; and if the reverse happen, namely, that the degree of civilization goes beyond the amount of freedom which the people possess, oppression is the consequence. . . . It is quite right that the governments of South America be free; but it is necessary that they should be so in the proportion stated; and the greatest triumph of our enemies would be to see us depart from that measure. . . . We . . . ought to introduce, gradually, such improvements as the country is prepared to receive, and for which its people are so well adapted by their docility and the tendency to improvement which mark their social character.

The expediency of San Martín's arguments remain largely unchallenged; their validity is subject to much debate.

San Martín assumed the mantle of Protector of Peru, promising that he would voluntarily relieve himself of that office once all royalist resistance was ended. To assist him in the affairs of government, he appointed three secretaries: Juan García del Río, Bernardo Monteagudo, and Hipólito Unánue, the meteorologist-physician. The Order of the Sun, a military fraternity, was founded. Though its immediate aim was to reward soldiers who had fought for independence, in effect it provided the basis for a military aristocracy. Another decree declared as free the children born of slave parents after July 28. Indians no longer had to pay tribute. Of lasting consequence was the establishment of a national library. If the rule of the Protector was despotic, it was also benevolent.

San Martín's strength was centered in and near Lima. In the mountains considerable royalist forces remained to threaten the existence of the new state. General Canterac descended from the mountains and approached the outskirts of Lima. Blocked by a clever maneuver of San Martín's, and with his flank suddenly turned, Canterac was forced towards the sea, towards Callao. There he relieved the royalist garrison, extracted as many supplies as he could and retreated towards the mountains. This was the moment when a little more daring and less caution might have completely smashed Canterac, but San Martín had ordered his lieutenants to avoid a pitched battle. His excessive caution aroused bitter resentment in the fiery Monteagudo and in other patriots.

Cochrane was furious, and chose this moment to engage in a violent quarrel with San Martín. He drew up a bill of complaints, one of which was that San Martín had failed to allot him his due portion of prize money; he also alleged that San Martín had unnecessarily withheld the regular pay due the crews of the fleet. Cochrane grabbed the public treasure being held at Ancón, paid his crews, and sailed for Chile. Just as San Martín had foreseen, the "child" had performed well but ultimately had proven to be quite troublesome. San Martín was left without a fleet.

Additional troubles were to descend without surcease upon the liberator. A military conspiracy led by Colonel Tomás Heres was easily crushed by San Martín, but the symptoms of dissatisfaction with his rule were growing.

Monteagudo was responsible for circulating rumors and for having hired men cry out in public places "Long live Emperor José!" in a malicious attempt to inflame public opinion against San Martín. In the Lautaro Society, which San Martín had founded in Lima, the members were mumbling and grumbling against the Protector. In the north, in the province of Guayaquil, the situation had become so serious that San Martín was compelled to journey there himself after having received the most disquieting and unsatisfactory news from his envoys.

The province of Guayaquil, with its very important port of the same name, had declared its independence from Peru not long after San Martín had landed. Three parties were in contention in Guayaquil: those who wished to declare their independence from Peru; those who supported the claim that Guayaquil properly belonged to Colombia; and a minority who wished to affiliate with Peru.

Deprived of a fleet, and with all these grave internal discords coming to a head almost simultaneously, San Martín concluded that he must form an alliance with the Great Liberator of the North. Consequently he set out for Guayaquil to meet with Simón Bolívar. To understand the drama of the encounter between the two great liberators of South America and the events that followed that interview, we must first turn to the tumultuous and stirring events that had been taking place in northern South America.

CHAPTER SEVEN

The Independence of Northern South America

THERE HAD BEEN A NUMBER OF UNSUCCESSFUL rebellions in the eighteenth century before the liberation movements in northern South America began. The success of the liberators is better comprehended by reviewing the activities of the precursors, as these early revolutionary figures have been called. In this brief survey reference will be made only to some of the outstanding men and events which crowd the pages of eighteenth-century Spanish America.

Two great Indian revolts, independent of each other but coexisting in time, shook the viceroyalties of New Granada and Peru in the years 1780–83. The cause of the revolt in Peru lay in the abuses the Indians suffered. They were being cheated by the corregidores, subjected to the merciless caprices of local priests, forced to toil in mines and fields under the most dreadful conditions. Notwithstanding the Bourbon reforms that were supposed to alleviate some of the wrongs, the Indians were as brutally exploited as ever. There seemed to be no hope for relief except through violence. Thus there was an unbroken series of plots, conspiracies, assassinations, and uprisings in the closing decades of colonial rule. The promise of reforms, only some of which had been carried out, stirred the hopes of the oppressed.

A widespread uprising that took years to suppress was initiated by Tupac Amarú, the Indian name assumed by José Gabriel Condorcanqui, so baptized on his birth in 1742. He was the son of an Indian chief and recognized as a lineal descendant of the Inca Tupac Amarú who had been executed by viceroy Toledo in 1571. At the time of the 1780 uprising, Tupac Amarú II was cacique, or chief, of a number of villages in the province of Tinta, viceroyalty of Peru, and was also Marquis of Oropesa, having been granted that title of Spanish nobility and all its privileges by Philip II.

The immediate cause of the revolt was the oppressive measures instituted by Aliaga, the corregidor of Tinta. He was a grossly cruel and greedy administrator. He had so aroused the wrath of the Church, with which he clashed over jurisdictional matters, that he had been excommunicated. Aliaga's abuse of the Indians was so outrageous that finally they resorted to arms. In November 1780, Tupac Amarú and a few followers captured the hated corregidor and ordered a public execution. To the assemblage gathered to witness the death of Aliaga, the Inca explained his drastic course of action. The Inca's bravely pronounced declaration that he would fight to eliminate abuses and the dramatic and audacious execution thus witnessed by the Indians produced an enthusiastic following. Initially the stated aim of the insurrection was to achieve redress of wrongs; in the course of the uprising the aim was radically changed to the independence of a restored Inca empire, with Tupac Amarú as emperor.

The uprising spread rapidly to a number of provinces, covering a vast area of what is now southern Peru, Bolivia, and the northwestern part of Argentina, and involving almost all the inhabitants. By March of the following year, Tupac Amarú commanded a fighting force of sixty thousand. A major battle ensued between the royalist army of seventeen thousand and the Inca's army in the middle of March, ending in the defeat of the rebels and the capture of the cacique and his family.

Areche, the royal visitador, pronounced a sentence of death for Tupac Amarú, his family, and all the leaders of the rebellion. There have been few examples in history of any more barbaric execution than the one carried out by the Spanish authorities. Before the astounded, mute throng of thousands, all the leaders and members of the Inca family had their tongues torn out, were strangled by the "iron screw," and hung.

Tupac and his wife were forced to witness all the bloody proceedings before they themselves were subjected to the excruciating tortures which preceded the *coup de grâce*. The heads of all the victims were cut off and were subsequently displayed in various towns. All the personal possessions of Tupac and his family were destroyed as

were all insignia which in any way might remind the Indians of their leader. The vindictiveness of the Spaniards
was matched by their foolishness in thus hoping to erase
the memory of the gallant Indian.

The insurrection, accompanied by additional vengeance
that reached new heights of horror, continued long after and
despite the execution of the Inca. In the next two years
that the rebels continued to fight, sometimes involving large
numbers of men in full-scale battles and sieges, it is estimated that eighty thousand Indians and Spaniards, mostly
the former, were killed, and whole towns and villages completely destroyed. Neither the "barbaric" Indians nor the
"civilized" Spaniards showed any mercy in their war of
extermination. The insurrection finally came to a halt,
though the Indians were not crushed.

The reforms that followed at the end of the insurrection
did little to placate the Indians. Without doubt, their
continuing hostility explains why many of them sided
against the chapetones when the Creoles began the struggle
for independence some thirty years later.

⟳

At about the same time that Peru was convulsed with
the Indian uprising, there was a rebellion in New Granada. Like the one led by Tupac Amarú, the revolt of the
comuneros, the commoners, began as a protest against
governmental abuses. In this instance the complaints centered on tax policies that Creoles especially resented. Spain,
like other colonial powers of the time, imposed upon her
colonies many taxes that were designed to support the

mother country. In 1780 the mounting costs of war with England led Spain to add more to a long list of burdensome taxes and to increase old ones. Here then is another link in the intricate web of the American Revolution and the colonial rivalries of western Europe. The grievance was aggravated by the arrogance of bureaucratic tax collectors, who earned the hatred of Creoles and Indians alike.

The center of resistance was in the province of Socorro, the principal manufacturing center of New Granada. One of the outstanding leaders of the revolt was Juan Francisco Berbeo, who led a strong military force of twenty thousand men to Bogotá, capital of the viceroyalty. The audiencia surrendered to the comuneros' demands to lighten some taxes, eliminate others, and correct other abuses. The victory was short-lived, however, for soon after the comuneros dissolved their militia and returned to their homes, the government reneged. The betrayal caught the comuneros completely unprepared to reorganize resistance against the royal troops, now rallied to enforce governmental authority. Some comuneros like José Antonio Galán, who had been suspicious of the original capitulation, continued to fight for several years, but the back of the revolt had been broken.

This revolt had another side, for in addition to the Creoles who participated in it, many Indians joined as allies, but for different aims. Excited by the reports of the early successes of the Tupac Amarú revolt, thousands of Indians throughout the northern area of the viceroyalty took up arms. Some of the Indians supported the comunero movement, whose leaders pledged to fight for alleviation of abuses. Others had more radical aims; they pledged allegiance to the Inca Tupac Amarú in the vain hope of achieving an independent Indian state.

Like the antitaxation struggles of the colonists in the thirteen English colonies, the comunero revolt did not aim at independence; but such struggles contributed to what eventually evolved into the more significant rebellion.

 ᑎᕼᑎ

Earlier we spoke of the influence of the French Revolution in the New World. One of the Creoles who had been impressed by many books of the Encyclopedists and by the political and social doctrines of the American and French revolutions was Antonio Nariño, born in Bogotá in 1760. The wealthy, learned Creole had been greatly impressed with Benjamin Franklin and adopted as his motto, "He snatched the lightning from the skies, and the scepter from the tyrant's hand."

His friendship with the viceroy of New Granada ended abruptly when the latter learned that Nariño had, in 1794, privately printed and distributed copies of the French *Declaration of the Rights of Man*. The bold principles enunciated in what was then a revolutionary document—principles still being fought for in the twentieth century by oppressed minorities everywhere—struck fear in the heart of the royal representative of the Spanish Crown. His fear was augmented by reports of the successful revolt of the blacks in Haiti and Santo Domingo. Such sedition shocked the royal authorities in New Granada. Would not such news coupled with the circulation of the inflammatory

French Declaration result in a similar threat to Spanish rule?

Nariño was arrested along with a number of persons charged with conspiracy. Nariño's defense stated that the *Declaration*'s principles had been printed before in Spanish books, and that the publication and circulation of the original were not criminal activities. Nevertheless he was condemned to ten years' imprisonment in Africa. En route, the ship bearing Nariño stopped at Cádiz. The prisoner escaped and managed to reach London after a short stay in Paris. In both these capitals Nariño endeavored to interest authorities—including William Pitt, the brilliant English prime minister—in promoting revolutionary enterprises in New Granada. Completely unsuccessful, the young Creole decided, in 1797, to return to Bogotá.

Entering Bogotá in disguise he was able to avoid detection, but not for long. He was captured and imprisoned until 1803, when he was released because of ill health. The next few years were spent in a sort of rural confinement, but his political activities were to be resumed when the revolutionary movement broke out anew in 1809.

⌒

The most illustrious of all the precursors was Francisco de Miranda. He was the son of wealthy Creole parents, born in Caracas, Venezula, on March 28, 1750. As a young man, after some college education, he showed an aptitude for military affairs. He was commissioned as a captain in the Spanish infantry in 1772, but it was not until 1780 that an opportunity arose to demonstrate his military abilities. In that year the North American patriots were still struggling to be free of the British colonial yoke when aid came rather unexpectedly from Spain. It has already been noted that the rivalries of the nations of western Europe affected the Spanish colonists in many ways. The close alliance, known as the Family Compact, between Spain and France led to the preparation of a joint expedition to attack some of the English dominions in the New World, taking advantage of England's preoccupation with the revolution in the thirteen North American colonies.

Miranda participated in the campaign that led to the capture of Pensacola, West Florida, and of the capital of the Bahama Islands. He rose to the rank of colonel, and was commissioned in 1781 to negotiate with the British in Jamaica and effect an exchange of prisoners of war. In 1783 he was charged with misconduct arising out of the Jamaican venture. He fled precipitously, taking refuge in the newly liberated United States of America, which had concluded a treaty of peace with England.

In the course of his travels in the new republic he became acquainted with many of that country's great men: Thomas Paine, Alexander Hamilton, Rufus King, and Henry Knox, among others. From the United States Miranda journeyed to Great Britain in 1785, then toured much of the European continent before returning for a prolonged stay in England. His mind was filled with a number of revolutionary projects that he presented to the members of several cabinets. Despite England's obvious interest in supporting plans to dismember the Spanish empire, none of Miranda's schemes was realized.

In 1790 he visited France in the hopes of gaining that revolutionary nation's support for a project to bring revolution to Spanish America. Not a man to waste time, Miranda became an officer in the French Army, comporting himself with such distinction in the war against Austria that he was promoted to brigadier general. General Dumouriez, under whom Miranda served, deserted to the enemy and the suspicions of the French revolutionary tribunal were directed at the Creole. Charged with complicity in Dumouriez's betrayal, he was imprisoned, released, imprisoned, released, and finally ordered into exile. He escaped and hid in Paris for several years.

Miranda departed from France in 1799 to stay in England, where he continued to formulate revolutionary plans that interested the English but were never realized. He came to the United States late in 1805, and there he finally gained support, albeit without official government cooperation, for a military expedition to Venezuela.

The Venezuelan patriot obtained enough financial backing to equip one vessel, the *Leander*, and two hundred venturesome Americans. The ship departed from New York City in February 1806 and proceeded to the British West Indies. After acquiring a few more recruits and provisioning two schooners, the invasion "fleet" sailed for the Venezuelan coast. The authorities there had been alerted by the Spanish Ambassador to the United States, who had almost complete knowledge of the expedition.

Miranda's expedition was a fiasco. His expectations that he need merely land on the coast and announce his presence, along with a call to revolution, for the citizens to rise and liberate themselves, had little basis in reality. He had had no direct contact with his country for more than twenty years, and it was quixotic to expect Venezuelans to respond spontaneously to the magic of his name. The expedition collapsed ingloriously. Miranda returned to England to plot, to write, and to circulate propaganda, to request aid from governments and from individuals, and to hope. In 1810, a not-too-surprised Miranda was called back to Venezuela to command the military forces of the revolution.

༄

That great vantage point, hindsight, enables historians to draw together the disparate threads of the past, manipulating them to create the whole cloth of momentous events. Spanish misrule, maltreatment of the Indians and Negroes, the expulsion of the Jesuits, the influence of the Enlightenment and of the American and French revolutions, the effects of continual local uprisings like that of the comuneros, the premature actions of a Miranda, the English invasion of Buenos Aires, the flowering of science, the growth of trade—all these and more constitute the causes, the preconditions, the events that on the historian's pages seem to converge ineluctably toward the one end: the emancipation of the Spanish colonies.

The actions leading to the independence of the colonies in northern South America were decisive in making permanent similar successes elsewhere in the New World. It may be reasonably conjectured that without the victories of Bolívar, who crushed the chief centers of Spanish military control, the independence of the other regions might have been short-lived. San Martín was not alone in estimating that the Spaniards had to be driven out of all of South America if any part of it was to remain permanently free of Spanish rule. In addition to the Spanish military power in the north, its rich silver and gold deposits were a principal source of economic strength. Therefore the prior military and political successes of the independence movements in La Plata and Chile might have been dissipated by the mother country if the northern colonies had continued as a base of operations. The Bolivarian campaigns guaranteed that any such hopes of Spanish recovery were illusory.

It has been already noted that the Napoleonic invasion of Spain produced a spirited resistance among the people, and that a temporary government committee, a Central Supreme Junta for all Spain, had been formed to lead the popular uprising against Napoleon in the name of the imprisoned Ferdinand VII. There were repercussions in all the colonies, and the solutions adopted independently in the various capitals and regions were somewhat similar. In Quito, capital of the presidency and audiencia of the province, part of the viceroyalty of New Granada, the Creoles refused to recognize the junta in Spain; they set up their own junta to rule in the name of Ferdinand. The Quito demand for self-government struck a responsive chord among Creoles elsewhere in the viceroyalty, although they were not unanimous about what specific steps to adopt. Some favored the compromise solution of sending delegates to the junta in Spain; others proposed that the viceroy call into being a junta for the entire viceroyalty. Sectional rivalries between Venezuela, Colombia, and Quito, however, prevented unity. Disagreements over questions of social reform and personal antagonisms contributed to temporarily dissipate a movement unconsciously heading for independence.

In Bogotá, the cabildo convinced the viceroy, Amar y Borbón, to summon an assembly of all the leading citizens in September 1809. While it was in session, the viceroy's troops liquidated the junta in Quito, before it had accomplished anything of consequence. Nor did the assembly in Bogotá accomplish much. The role played by the brilliant Creole Camilio Torres is of historic interest, however. He drew up the complaints of the Creoles in a treatise entitled *A Memorial of Grievances and Rights*. That paper, along with Torres' subsequent writings, became the first basic documents of Colombian independence.

The lack of unity among the dissidents made it relatively easy for the viceroy, the intendants, the upper clergy, the Holy Office, the judges of the audiencias, the wealthy Spanish merchants, and other peninsulars comprising the top colonial officialdom to restore their authority. Nevertheless, what had been set in motion could not be completely halted. The climate was conducive not only to the circulation of revolutionary ideas, but to attempts to carry them out.

In Caracas, capital of the captaincy-general of Venezuela, a political subdivision of New Granada, dissatisfied Creoles had been meeting secretly for years in the Sociedad Patriótica. Ostensibly a debating society, its members had in fact discussed and planned a revolutionary uprising to take place when the opportunity should arise. When it became known that a police spy had reported its clandestine meetings, disguised as card parties, the patriots decided on immediate and bold action, making providential use of their membership in the Caracas cabildo.

On Holy Thursday, April 19, 1810, the cabildo members were gathered to attend church. In the square, outside the church, they confronted Don Vicente Emparán, the governor of Venezuela, and demanded that he turn over his authority to a junta. Seeking to delay and taking advantage of the fact that it was Holy Thursday, the governor stated that he would give the matter his careful consideration after attending mass. However, he was led out of the church by one of the conspirators, who held a knife to his ribs and escorted the shocked official to the meeting hall in the city's main plaza. There an enthusiastic crowd listened to revolutionary speeches and learned that the governor had been deposed and his authority assumed by a twenty-three-man junta, the first independent government in South America. Emparán stoically accepted the inevitable; he permitted himself to be escorted to the port of La Guaira, where he embarked for Spain.

In Colombia, within a few months, juntas were established in the commercial and mining centers, the principal towns and cities of the viceroyalty.

Appeals for unity, whether programmatic or political, came to naught. For many decades there had been intense competition among the various regions comprising the huge viceroyalty. At the moment when common aims should have been the overriding consideration, the past rivalries were revived, to the disadvantage of the revolutionary movement. These rivalries were economic and social in nature: competition among the several ports and conflict of interests between ranchers and commercial and mining proprietors.

Narrow local patriotisms based on pride of city or of province or on support of local caudillos produced antagonisms that interfered seriously with any concept of nationalism. In fact, it was apparent that several nationalisms were emerging. Not only was the revolutionary movement hampered, but one may discern the outlines for the eventual division of the viceroyalty into the contemporary states with boundaries corresponding to the old colonial subdivisions.

Each regional faction sought its own path to independence, but these paths were to cross in the course of the revolution. That they did so was due in large measure to the leadership of Simón Bolívar. Originally concerned only with the cause of Venezuela, Bolívar was destined to become the liberator of much more.

⤷

Simón José Antonio de la Santíssima Trinidad de Bolívar y Palacios, so baptized on July 24, 1783, was the son of extremely wealthy Creoles, members of one of the most distinguished families of the Venezuelan colony. On his father's side, Simón's American ancestry went back to 1578, when the first Bolívar came to the Americas, and his mother could also claim descent from a long line of wealthy

Creoles. Simón was orphaned early in life; his father died in 1786 and his mother in 1792. As the heir to one of the largest fortunes of any family in South America—several houses, agricultural estates, large herds of cattle, rich copper mines—it did not seem likely that he was destined to become the great revolutionary leader, the man more responsible than any other for freeing Spanish South America.

Bolívar had little formal education, but a succession of private tutors provided him with a splendid and most unusual education. The two outsanding tutors who profoundly influenced Bolívar were Andrés Bello and Simón Rodríguez. Bello became South America's most distinguished man of letters and was the founder of modern Spanish grammar. Rodríguez, pseudonym for Carreño, was an unusual educator, a revolutionary with great vision, equipped with an extraordinary knowledge of the classics and of the writings of the men of the Enlightenment. Thus Bolívar became acquainted with the philosophy and political thinking of the Englishmen Hobbes and Locke, and with the great French writers of the Age of Reason— Voltaire, Rousseau, Montesquieu, Condillac, and many others. His education in the classics was not neglected, but Bolívar preferred the philosophers and political theorists of more recent vintage; his favorite author was Voltaire, the brilliant satirist and philosopher who influenced generations of great minds. Cervantes' fictional immortal, Don Quixote—who struggled to right wrongs in a world filled with injustices—profoundly affected the real man of the world who set out to liberate a portion of it. In his later

years Bolívar was to comment wryly that "the three greatest
idiots in the world were Jesus Christ, Don Quixote, and
myself."

Part of his education was obtained abroad, as was the
custom for the sons of many wealthy American families. In
the United States he interviewed prominent citizens and
toured the battle sites of the American Revolution. The
experience probably had lasting influence. In Madrid,
where he arrived in 1799, a storybook romance developed
between the young Simón and the even younger María
Teresa, daughter of the Marquis of Toro. After a whirlwind courtship, he married and returned with his bride to
Venezuela. Not long after, in 1803, his young wife died.
The tragedy affected Simón so deeply that he vowed he
would never remarry.

The death of his wife was crucial in a more significant
sense. Some twenty-five years later Bolívar said:

I loved my wife very much. . . . If my wife had not died,
I would not have made my second trip to Europe. It is probable that there would not have been born . . . the ideas which
I acquired in my travels; in America I should not have gained
the experience nor should I have made that study of the world,
of men, and of affairs which has served me so well during the
entire course of my political career. The death of my wife
placed me at an early age in the road of politics: it caused me
to follow the chariot of Mars instead of the plow of Ceres.

In 1804 Bolívar returned to Madrid; we have already
noted that he was ordered to depart ignominiously along
with other "foreigners."

From Spain Bolívar proceeded to Paris, the city of lights

and gaiety, of enlightenment and entertainment. Bolívar partook plentifully of both. The young traveler encountered Rodríguez, his former tutor, now a political exile earning his living by teaching Spanish. With Rodríguez as guide and mentor, Bolívar traveled throughout Italy. While touring Rome, they visited historic Aventine Hill and at Monte Sacro Bolívar passionately pledged,

I swear before you, I swear before the God of my fathers; by my fathers themselves, by my honor and by my country, that my arm shall not rest nor my mind be at peace until I have broken the chains which bind me, by the will and power of Spain.

It was not an oath carelessly made by a romantic youth on the spur of the moment. The pledge was recalled many years later by Bolívar in a letter he sent to Rodríguez. It was a pledge seriously made, and more seriously fufilled.

᠊ᦂ᠊

Bolívar returned to Venezuela in 1807. He joined with the revolutionists who were active in the Sociedad Patriótica, preparing for the opportune moment to overthrow the governor; it came on April 19, 1810, as has been already related.

Shortly after coming into power, the new junta sent diplomatic agents to London: Simón Bolívar, Andrés Bello, and Luis López Méndez. The British government could not receive the mission officially—England was still at war with Napoleon and Spain was a valued ally. Any desire to reap advantages from successful revolutions in Spanish

America had to be subordinated to the priority of defeating Napoleon. Yet the English were quite friendly, ignoring the angry recriminations of the Spanish Embassy.

During the mission's extended stay in London, Bolívar spent a considerable amount of time with Miranda. Despite Miranda's ignominious failure in 1806, Bolívar still respected the military ability of the famous precursor, and convinced him to return to Venezuela, where they arrived, separately, in the fall of 1810.

During the year 1810 and for most of 1811 the royalists had done little to contain the developing insurgencies. The Supreme Junta in Spain was much too preoccupied with the war on the peninsula to be able to send aid to New Granada. The patriots had time to consolidate and spread the revolution throughout the provinces. Following the successful uprising in Caracas revolts took place in New Granada, where independent juntas arose in a number of the provinces: Cartagena, Antioquía, Socorro, Cundinamarca (where Nariño assumed the leadership) and elsewhere. (However, the royalists crushed the movements in Popayán and on the Isthmus of Panama.) Declarations of independence were proclaimed, provisional governments formed, and regional and personal rivalries proliferated. For a while, almost four years, there were three main insurgent governments: Nariño was president of the state of Cundinamarca, the central province with Bogotá as its capital; a congress presided over the United Provinces of New Granada, with its seat at Cartagena on the coast (and was constantly at odds with Nariño); and a congress ruled in Venezuela, which proceeded on its own path of revolutionary liberation. In a number of areas independent juntas continued to operate, compounding the confusion.

In Venezuela, Miranda was elected to the congress, where he argued effectively in favor of absolute independence. On July 5, 1811, the congress voted in favor of Miranda's proposal, proclaiming the country's independence. A constitution was completed on December 21. It reflected the economic interests of the Creoles and contained some aspects of political democracy. Expressions of social progress were limited on at least two counts: Negro slavery was perpetuated; and no guarantees were incorporated to make effective the declaration that all people—except Negro slaves—were equal. On the positive side, the tributes the Indians had been forced to pay were abolished.

Independence had been proclaimed, but it had yet to be achieved. Royalists had retained control over two separate areas of the coastal region of Venezuela: the extreme northeastern coast and its northwestern counterpart, including the ports of Coro and Maracaibo. An unusual opportunity was gratuitously presented to the royalist forces commanded by Domingo Monteverde in the form of a devastating earthquake that convulsed Caracas and neighboring towns on Holy Thursday, March 28, 1812.

Coming in the afternoon when large numbers of people were in church and the troops were in barracks, the shocks took an enormous toll in lives and property. In the midst of the ruins, among the dead and dying, members of the clergy were quick to inform the people that the quake was an expression of the wrath of God: "the scourge of an irritated Deity against the innovators who had rejected the most virtuous of monarchs, Ferdinand VII, the Lord's anointed." Bolívar, who was feverishly lending aid to the victims of the quake, is reported to have shouted: "If nature is against us, we will fight against that too, and make it do what we want."

Strangely enough, none of the towns in royalist hands was affected by the catastrophe. Monteverde seized the opportunity to commence a campaign, starting from the northwest and moving toward the republican-held center.

Monteverde's initial successes threw the republican government into panic. It gave supreme power to General Miranda, creating in effect a military dictatorship. No one seemed to object to the dictatorship, but Miranda was not at all popular. There were desertions, some officers and men going over to the royalists. Bolívar, now a colonel, was shunted off by Miranda to defend Puerto Cabello. Within the town antirepublican elements aided royalist troops to capture the stronghold; Bolívar and forty of his men barely managed to escape to La Guaira.

Miranda was completely disheartened. Maybe he was too old for vigorous campaigning, or maybe the succession of royalist victories unnerved him; perhaps he was discouraged by his inability to maintain unity and discipline in the face of adversity, or disillusioned with the indifference exhibited by many inhabitants. The strange truth is that Miranda decided that the declaration of independence was premature, and without consulting any of his officers or members of the government, he suddenly surrendered on July 25. Even while Monteverde was approaching Caracas, Miranda fled to La Guaira, abandoning his troops and his country. Alexander Scott, an American envoy on hand to supervise the distribution of food for the quake-stricken inhabitants, called Miranda's extraordinary conduct "a shameful and treacherous capitulation."

Miranda intended to embark on a British ship that was waiting for him in the harbor of La Guaira. The general had all his personal belongings, including a large sum of gold that was the property of the Venezuelan government, put aboard. He chose to spend the night on shore since the ship was not to sail before dawn. That decision cost him his freedom. An outraged Bolívar and several officers stole into Miranda's quarters and arrested the sleeping general. Now Bolívar committed an action that, like Miranda's, has been subject to much criticism and speculation. He turned Miranda over to the royalists. The fallen dictator was shipped to Spain, there to languish in prison in Cádiz until his death in 1816.

Bolívar and other Venezuelan officers were imprisoned by Monteverde. Some were shot, some escaped to rejoin the revolutionary movement. Through the intervention of powerful friends, Bolívar was granted a passport to leave the country; Monteverde did not consider the young Creole an important enough person to warrant holding him. Bolívar sailed to Curaçao. Many patriots took refuge on other islands, while some escaped into the interior. The first Venezuelan republic had come to an inglorious end. The Spanish colony was reconstituted with Monteverde directing an unprecedented reign of terror.

It was clear now to Bolívar that Venezuela could not be independent unless Spain was defeated on the battlefield.

Nor could Venezuela remain independent unless Spanish arms were driven out of all northern South America. As long as a Spanish military force of any size existed in the provinces, pronouncements of independence were just so much paper and talk.

It was abundantly clear, too, that Spanish armed forces were able to count on support from various elements of the population. Recent events had shown that some patriots were "summer soldiers," unable to withstand adversity; many inhabitants were utterly indifferent to the cause of independence, notably the Negro slaves, the Indians, and even some Creoles; some were loyal to local caudillos whose concept of freedom meant fighting for the liberation of their own locality, their personal freedom, not to be restricted by Creoles, chapetones, or by any authority; and some Creoles were fanatically loyal to Spain.

Furthermore the immense task of liberation became all the more difficult by virtue of the serious dissensions, reaching the proportions of open warfare, within the patriot ranks. Added to these difficulties were the normal problems of training recruits, obtaining finances, arms, munitions, and other provisions for the insurgent armies. Finally, it must be noted that, unlike their North American counterparts who had secured significant help from France and Spain, the Spanish American patriots had to achieve the liberation of their countries without official aid from any of the great powers.

In the fall of 1812 Bolívar left Curaçao for Cartagena, where the patriot government of New Granada was still operating. Bolívar offered his services to that government and urged it to come to the support of the Venezuelan cause. In a *Manifesto to the Citizens of New Granada* Bolívar argued against a defensive war. The best way to defend New Granada, he wrote, would be to take the offensive against the Spaniards and help to liberate Venezuela. He appealed for unity among the provinces within the New Granadan confederation. But his plea fell on deaf ears. New Granada, even more than Venezuela, was hopelessly divided into factions; centralists who favored a strong central government fought federalists who favored a federation of provinces, each with considerable political autonomy.

This political divisiveness, typical of most of the Latin American regions—Argentina, Chile, Venezuela, the New Granadan area, and Mexico—continued to interfere with the independence movement and lasted for decades afterwards, in some instances prevailing to this day. It is one of the principal reasons for the weak governments that characterized many of the Latin American republics through much of their turbulent history.

Only a few leaders, like Camilio Torres, saw the wisdom of Bolívar's proposals. They had enough power to obtain for Bolívar command of a small force with which he won a number of engagements along the northeastern region of Colombia, driving the royalists out of the area of the lower Magdalena, the Valley of Cúcuta and the border town of Cúcuta itself. These successes prompted the New Granadan congress to commission Bolívar to invade Venezuela. For the first time soldiers from Colombia were to fight in Venezuela in the common cause of liberation. In the spring of 1813 Bolívar's troops freed most of the western area of Venezuela.

During the campaign, in June, Bolívar issued a bloody proclamation of war to the death—*guerra a muerte!* In the decree, he warned:

> Any Spaniard who does not, by every active and effective means, work against tyranny in behalf of this just cause, will be considered an enemy and punished; as a traitor to the nation, he will inevitably be shot by a firing squad. . . .

Bolívar's drastic decision was a reaction to the wanton acts of cruelty by the bloodthirsty José Tomás Boves, a Spanish officer who commanded a band of llaneros, semisavage plainsmen of Venezuela. Like the early gaucho of Argentina, the huaso of Chile, the vaquero of Mexico, these cowboys of Venezuela—mostly mulattoes and mestizos— were expert horsemen, lawless and seminomadic; they loved to fight, and their skill as lancers and their superb horsemanship threw fear into their enemies. To llaneros anyone was an enemy who threatened any limitation of their primitive freedom, their simple understanding of personal freedom. With Boves at their head, the llaneros burned estates, raped, looted, massacred inhabitants, and never took prisoners of war.

Bolívar intended to be merciless against such acts of cruelty and the known brutalities of the Spaniards, justifying his actions in the name of the cause of independence.

Caracas was recaptured by the patriots in August 1813. The cabildo of the city proclaimed the conquering hero Captain General of the Venezuelan army and awarded him the title of Liberator, the title that Bolívar always valued above all. At the time, however, the title was premature. Venezuela was to be reconquered by the royalists once more.

Royalist troops moved towards the center of Venezuela, from the northeast, east and southeast. In February 1814 Boves with seven thousand lancers literally wiped out a republican force of three thousand. Where Creoles were involved, Boves set out on a deliberate policy of extermination; the Creole inhabitants of towns and villages occupied by Boves' men were massacred. In retaliation Bolívar ordered that over eight hundred Spanish prisoners who had vainly attempted to escape from the prison at La Guaira be executed.

At La Puerta, Boves with a force of five thousand lancers and three thousand infantry defeated a republican force of twenty-three hundred led by Bolívar; half the rebels were killed. Valencia surrendered to Boves, who failed to keep the terms of the surrender. Cracking a whip, he ordered the terrified women to dance, while in a nearby field all the men who had been rounded up were "lanced as if they had been bulls."

Defense of Caracas seemed hopeless. In early July Bolívar ordered its evacuation. Thousands of men, women, and children trudged a dreadful 150 miles to Barcelona. Near Barcelona, eight thousand royalists under the command of Morales, a lieutenant of Boves, caught up with and defeated Bolívar and his force of three thousand. Morales ordered the throats cut of all prisoners and of all the inhabitants of the town of Aragua de Barcelona; a thousand taking refuge in the church were thus barbarously murdered. Massacre after massacre took place as towns were taken by the royalists.

Bolívar fled, finally reaching the safety of Cartagena. He left a Venezuela despoiled and ravaged by the war. A Spanish official wrote,

There are no more provinces left. Towns which had thousands of inhabitants are now reduced to a few hundreds or even a few dozen. Of others, there are nothing but vestiges, to show that they were once inhabited by human beings. Roads and fields are full of unburied corpses; whole villages have been burnt; whole families are nothing but a memory. . . . Agriculture has stopped, and in the towns they are short of the most essential articles of food.*

On reaching Cartagena, Bolívar found the United Provinces in the midst of civil strife; Cundinamarca was forcibly resisting the Granadan government. Bolívar was entrusted with the command of a contingent that marched on the Cundinamarcan capital, Bogotá, and compelled the city's defenders to surrender. That victory brought the central province firmly under the control of the New Granadan federation. Gratefully the congress proclaimed Bolívar as Captain General of the armed forces. But the elation of the government and of Bolívar was short-lived.

Royalist forces mounted a series of offensives that the Captain General was unable to counter. He complained of inadequate support from the government, which was still suffering from internal rifts. Furthermore, the patriots

---

* J. B. Trend, *Bolívar and the Independence of Spanish America* (New York, 1968), p. 88.

were unable to cope with the large numbers of royalist sympathizers who took advantage of every opportunity to harass them and subvert authority. Since Bolívar felt that his effectiveness was hampered by the constant bickerings of the government leaders, he resigned his command and exiled himself to Jamaica in May 1815.

The month before, large detachments of reinforcements from Spain reached Venezuelan shores and were proceeding to New Granada. The war with Napoleon was over, Ferdinand had been restored to the throne, the liberal Constitution of 1812 was discarded, and the monarchy was now in a position to take positive steps to recover its losses in the New World. The decision was to concentrate first on subduing the northern provinces of South America, the most important possessions economically. The expedition was commanded by General Pablo Morillo, who had distinguished himself during the campaigns against the French.

By the spring of 1816 the Spanish army had reconquered the northern provinces. The New Granadan government was dissolved in 1816; only isolated pockets of resistance remained in both Venezuela and New Granada. Morillo instituted a military government in the area that had previously been the viceroyalty.

To punish the patriots and to paralyze any rebel activity, the new military government unleashed another reign of terror. The property of patriots was confiscated and the patriots themselves executed. To the pleas of the women and children Morillo answered, "Your fathers, your sons, brothers or husbands have been traitors to the king; therefore they ought to lose their property and their lives."

Camilio Torres and Francisco José de Caldas (the great savant), to name but two of the many patriot leaders, were summarily executed. Patriots who did not incur the death penalty were persecuted in a number of ways; some were imprisoned, some condemned to heavy labor—paving streets and building roads and bridges—without pay, yet they had to provide their own food. Wives of patriot leaders were chained; priests were fettered, maltreated, exiled; mutilated bodies placed on pikes grimly decorated plazas and roads. The terror lasted for months, but instead of inspiring fear, it renewed the hatred of the colonials for the Spanish tyrants. If reconciliation had been at all contemplated, it was made impossible by such harsh measures.

The liberation struggles continued while Bolívar was in exile. The Spanish regime rested on a precarious foundation, for it had to face relentless and extensive guerrilla warfare. This is the most difficult to contain, as it defies the normal conduct of military operations. Based on the support of the people, exasperatingly elusive and avoiding large-scale confrontations, a constant source of harassment, inflicting small but steady losses upon the armed forces, sporadically raiding in dozens of locales, magically appearing in the most unlikely places and at the most unlikely times, always an example to the discontented—the many guerrilla bands prevented the Spaniards from establishing a stable regime. Only the capitals were secure.

During his stay in Jamaica Bolívar reviewed the past years of political and military struggle. Much of his thought is expressed in his famous Jamaican letter—a portion of which is quoted (page 32)—which evidenced a new orientation toward the liberation movement and a prophetic vision. He now viewed as utopian previous concepts about a united South American nation. Just as Moreno had deliberated about the impossibility of one South American government, Bolívar also argued that "varied climates, diverse situations, contrary interest, and dissimilar characteristics divide America." Economic, geographic and psychological factors precluded the creation of one vast domain. He considered the state of South America "to be similar to that after the fall of the Roman Empire, when each part of the wreckage formed a political system conforming to its needs, or was led by the ambition of some chief, family, or association." Infinitely more feasible, he argued, would be the construction of fifteen to seventeen republics. A republican form of government, modeled somewhat on the English parliamentary system, would be most suitable; at the same time Bolívar gave strong arguments against the federalist type of republic after having seen its ineffectiveness in Venezuela. That which was efficient in the United States of America was not automatically applicable to the South American nations.

Although one huge nation was neither possible nor advisable, Bolívar projected the vision of a fraternity of the many nations of the New World, to be encouraged by the formation of a Pan American Congress. He predicted, with extraordinary accuracy, that some of the nations would establish monarchies, that life-term presidencies would come into existence, that an oligarchy would evolve in Chile, that there would be irreconcilable conflict in Mexico between the aristocratic elements and the mass of the people, that canals should and would be constructed across the Isthmus of Panama; and he dreamed that the New World offered the distant prospect of a new race, an amalgamation of all the races to form a new homogeneous people.

From Jamaica, Bolívar went to Haiti. At first Alexandre Pétion, the president of the first black republic, was rather cool to Bolívar's requests for aid. He was disturbed by the failure of the South American revolutionary leaders to take any action to free the numerous Negro slaves. The liberty-loving Creoles who showed themselves capable of the greatest sacrifices gave no consideration to the plight of the slaves. Nor had much thought been given to the need for social reforms that would ameliorate the conditions of the Indians, the mestizos, the mulattoes, the zambos. They were just so many pawns to be recruited by patriots and royalists to fight for a cause which had no profound significance to them. To be subjects of a Spanish empire or subjects of independent American nations governed by Creoles did not make much difference. Slaves exploited in the mines or on the plantations had little to gain whichever side won. There was little hope or promise of basic economic, political, and social change.

Pétion's reluctance was perfectly understandable. He finally pledged aid only on the condition that Bolívar take immediate steps to abolish slavery. The Liberator accepted the condition; when he implemented the promise shortly after returning to the mainland, the rewards were great for the patriot armies.

In the early spring of 1816 Bolívar set out from Haiti

with a small expeditionary force for Venezuela. After landing on the island of Margarita, where some new recruits were added, they reached the mainland and futilely attempted to arouse a still apathetic populace. An encounter with royalist forces led to a rout, and once again Bolívar was forced to flee his homeland for the temporary safety of Haiti. From September until December, Bolívar was busy obtaining material aid from both the Haitian government and from a wealthy Venezuelan exile, Louis Brion. Preparations completed, the indomitable Liberator returned to the mainland, this time to stay until complete victory over Spain was ensured.

⌇

Bolívar's carefully thought-out decision to invade the northeastern area of Venezuela turned out to be most fortuitous. This region is the Venezuelan part of Guiana, through which the lower portion of the Orinoco River flows. In its plains guerrilla fighting had been going on for a year under the leadership of the mestizo José Antonio Páez.

A vivid characterization and description of Páez was given by Daniel Florencio O'Leary, an Irish volunteer who became Bolívar's aide-de-camp:

. . . of medium height, robust, and well-formed, though the lower part of his body did not match his big torso; chest and shoulders very wide; a short neck held up by a bulky head covered with dark chestnut hair, short and kinky, a round bear; lively brown eyes; straight nose with wide apertures, thick lips. . . . Wholly illiterate, he was ignorant of the theory

of the military profession which he had followed so long. . . .
As a guerrilla leader he was unparalleled. . . . Without being
bloodthirsty, he did not economize on bloodshed. . . . His
ambition was without limits. He wanted power, but absolute
power, the power of caprice and abuse. Ambition and greed
were his dominant passions.

Páez was to play a prominent role in Venezuelan politics
long after the revolution. He was president, and controlled
presidents, from 1830 to 1846, and was actual dictator of
Venezuela from 1861 to 1863.

After Boves' death in 1814, Páez had managed to win
over many of the llaneros to the patriot cause. The ex-cow-
boy was an astute, fearless, audacious, cruel leader—the
only kind acceptable to the llaneros. They joyfully followed
him in an endless series of hit-and-run raids that drove
Spanish generals like Morillo wild with rage and frustration. During the year 1816, before Bolívar's arrival in the
province, Páez kept royalist troops busy along the upper
Orinoco and Apure rivers, making the Liberator's task that
much easier. By July 1817 the royalists had evacuated
Angostura, an important trading center on the Orinoco,
some 270 miles from the delta. The independence forces
were now in control of the province of Guiana.

At Angostura (present-day Ciudad Bolívar) the Liberator
set up headquarters and established the provisional capital
of the Venezuelan government. Other than some sporadic
minor engagements, the following months until early 1819
were spent in political organization, recruiting, and training.

Particularly important was the recruiting of a considerable number of international volunteers. The first large contingent of five regiments, superbly equipped, left England in December 1817. Over a period of the next five years, volunteers totaling about six thousand officers and men arrived in South America. Most were English, Irish, and Scots with a sprinkling of Germans, Poles, French, Americans, and Italians.

Such soldiers of fortune as these had mixed motives for volunteering their services; money lured some, as adventure and glory did others; some professional soldiers were attracted by the prospects of hard fighting and the hope of rising in the ranks; others dreamed of settling on an estate in an exotic, rich land after victory had been gained; and undoubtedly there were many who firmly espoused the cause for which the South American patriots were fighting. It is most probable that the psychological and material motivations were least significant. International volunteers almost always have chosen the cause of humanity. Some examples that come readily to mind are the Europeans who volunteered to fight on the side of the American revolutionists in the eighteenth century; the international volunteers who espoused the cause of Republican Spain against Fascism in 1936–39; Europeans and Americans who rendered heroic service to the Chinese against Japan prior to the beginning of World War II; the American pilots who flew for England in 1939–41 before the entry of their country in the war. The volunteers who flocked to Bolívar's banner were of that same worthy breed.

It is doubtful that any of the volunteers envisioned the

hardships they would encounter, unlike any experienced in the most severe European campaigns of the Napoleonic Wars, of which many were veterans. In the first place they were unused to the food. The staple was *tasajo*—a dried, jerked beef of the consistency of rawhide, which could keep indefinitely when salted; unfortunately salt often was in short supply. Dysentery was a common scourge which decimated the effective fighting strength of the volunteers. Much worse were the effects of tropical diseases, with yellow fever taking special toll of those who came from northern climes. The bites of insects took an additional toll; the bites of chiggers left infected sores, dangerous pockets of pus sometimes so seriously affecting the unfortunate victim that amputation of a foot, leg, or arm might be necessary. A common infection, called the *maldita*, resulted from an insect bite and created an ulcerous condition that penetrated to the bone.

Most of the legionaries who came from the British Isles originally wore resplendent uniforms. In the tropics such clothing was unsuitable, and as it rotted through wear, dirt, and the course of time, many of the soldiers were reduced to wearing the same simple costumes as their brothers-in-arms; often that meant going about semi-naked. Officers—even colonels—who had but one shirt were compelled to wash it themselves; when the river was infested with alligators, one officer would stand guard while his comrades did their laundering. Complaints were useless, especially in view of the fact that the patriots endured precisely the same hardships; no favoritism was shown.

Of the six thousand volunteers, not more than 150 survived until the end of the wars. Most had been killed or died of privations, while some had deserted. It is estimated that the actual number engaging in any one campaign did not exceed twelve hundred. Yet it is reasonable to assume that the presence of the foreign volunteers made for a considerable difference in determining the outcome of the most decisive battles in the years 1819 to 1824. The largest force commanded by Bolívar in any one battle did not exceed sixty-five hundred—at the second, and famous, Battle of Carabobo in which the foreign legions distinguished themselves. Such numbers more or less correspond with the forces commanded by George Washington (except at the battle of Yorktown, when he led a force of eight thousand Continentals reinforced by eight thousand Frenchmen). In such engagements the addition of a few hundred men often meant the difference between victory or defeat. The role of the foreign legions ought not to be underestimated.

It is a tribute to Bolívar's genius as a leader of men that he was able to whip together some semblance of discipline, to make an effective fighting army out of such diverse units as Páez's fierce llaneros, the foreign legionaries speaking so many strange tongues, and the thousands of South Americans from every class and caste that made up the bulk of his forces.

To the congress assembled at Angostura in February 1819 Bolívar delivered an eloquent and lengthy message that incorporated his political and military plans. His political thought echoed much of the libertarian doctrines of the French Revolution, clearly evidenced in his defense of the rights of man—freedom of action, thought, and speech. On the other hand the English parliamentary system was the institutional model that he proposed in modified from. Government should be based on the sovereignty of the people. Because of the special conditions characterizing the evolution of Spanish South America—geography, climate, the varied peoples, and the lack of democratic experience —the republic should have an hereditary senate along with a lower house of representatives chosen by popular election, and a life-term president.

Bolívar's political theory had little bearing on the decisions of the congress, which was concerned with more pressing, practical problems. At the moment independence was only a theory. A war had yet to be fought and won. Members of the congress may have had hesitations over some of Bolívar's political recommendations, but they were agreed on his military proposals. His plans were accepted and he was appointed commander-in-chief of all the Venezuelan forces.

Bolívar intended to free Venezuela by proceeding across its jungles, plains, marshes, crossing the Arauca River, then up and over the Andes to attack the royalists in New Granada before returning to Venezuela from its west. It was an audacious plan, but not so far-fetched as it might seem. Bolívar could count on some seventy-two hundred men in Venezuela, whereas Morillo commanded fourteen thousand. In New Granada, Bolívar assumed that he would be able to gain additional forces, namely those already

engaged in guerrilla warfare plus new recruits. And in
New Granada the royalists were spread out, with about
four thousand men along the northeastern frontier and another three thousand widely dispersed along the coast and
in the interior. By marching westward first, Bolívar expected to avoid the main body of Morillo's army; whereas
in New Granada the patriots would be able to concentrate
larger masses against the widely dispersed royalist groups.

Páez and some of the llaneros were left to harass Morillo
in Venezuela, while Bolívar with the main body moved
westward towards New Granada. Then followed days and
nights of the most tortured marching through the marshes,
across a network of rivers swollen with the spring rains,
the men beset by swarms of mosquitos and other insects,
plodding through mud and incessant rain, eating poorly
roasted and unsalted meat—more than a thousand miles
of nightmare. At the small town of Tamé, the exhausted
men were permitted to rest a few days before undertaking
an even more nightmarish journey. Reinforced by Granadan troops numbering about 1,400 led by the Colombian
general Francisco de Paula Santander, Bolívar set out to
cross the towering Andes.

In the annals of military history, only the feat of Hanni-
bal crossing the Alps and San Martín's crossing of the
southern Andes match Bolívar's spectacular crossing of
the northern cordilleras. Used to the hot climate of the
plains, with its hardships of heat and insects and alligators
and rain, the llaneros were awestruck and overwhelmed by
the grandeur of the seemingly impassable snow-covered
peaks. The route chosen was the famed Pisba Pass, through

which they could reach the high Colombian plateau. After having passed through the foothills, they reached the base of the last peak, soaring 10,000 feet into the clouds. On July 4 they commenced the difficult climb. The first hazard was to ford a number of mountain torrents, made the worse by rains and bitter wind. For much of the ascent the men had to plod through cold, thick mud. They struggled over rocky crags and teetered on the edges of crevasses; a few men slipped down into the bottomless abysses. Almost all suffered from dysentery. Horses and mules collapsed, not one surviving the trip. The extreme altitude caused men to struggle for breath and to suffer from the soroche— the dread mountain illness. Cases of severe frostbite were common, and many soldiers froze to death; the English lost almost one-fourth of their complement. The few women camp followers endured every hardship most stoically, and it is recorded that several even gave birth in those terrible circumstances.

That night, the straggling army huddled around a few, pitiful camp fires which afforded scant relief to the fierce wind and even fiercer cold. In the early dawn they set out once again to climb until at last they reached the cloud-covered summit. They had marched over incredibly difficult terrain for more than a month, two weeks of which had been spent in ascending the Andes. Never before had any individuals, much less an army, succeeded in crossing the Pisba during the rainy season. The men vowed they would rather die in combat than to have to retreat over that hellish route.

They began the difficult descent, finally reaching Socha,

some 1500 feet below the pass. There the men rested and were showered with gifts from the overjoyed inhabitants of the region. Their spirits revived and their supplies of animals and food replenished, the men were eager to come to grips with the enemy. They fell upon the royalists in the Vargas swamp. It was not at all a decisive battle; the number of men lost on both sides was small. But it was an important one in that for the first time a large royalist force was on the defensive. Bolívar suffered one irreparable loss when Colonel Rooke, a very brave and efficient officer of the British legion, died. He had been wounded in the arm; immediately after its amputation he waved his severed arm in the air and shouted "Long live the fatherland!" To the query "Which one?" he replied that his was the country in which he was buried. He died a few days later.

From the Vargas swamp, the Bolivarians proceeded towards Tunja, in the Valley of Boyacá. There, at the bridge of Boyacá, the most decisive battle of the independence movement of Colombia and Venezuela took place on August 7, 1819. General Barreiro was hurrying back to join the viceroy's forces in Bogotá, but the patriot army's rapid movement had compelled him to set up a weak defense at the River Boyacá. The British attacked the center, General Santander moved in from the left, and the llaneros, who had forded the stream, attacked the royalists from the rear. Almost completely surrounded, the royalist force was overwhelmed by the tactics and the extraordinary heroism of the patriots. General Barreiro surrendered after a battle that lasted no more than two hours yet won New Granada. Many of the prisoners were Granadans; swayed by Bolívar's eloquence or convinced that the patriots were on the winning side, they joined the Liberator's army.

The news of the Battle of Boyacá so disconcerted the viceroy that he fled for his life before the end of the day. Bolívar rode into Bogotá the day afterward, making a triumphant entry to the cheers of the inhabitants welcoming their hero.

During the next few weeks, the Spanish administrators of the provinces of New Granada fled, leaving the country to the patriots. Some mop-up operations of little consequence were all that remained to liberate the vast territory. After putting Santander in charge of the armed forces, Bolívar made his way back to Angostura, where he was greeted by the population as the liberator and father of his country.

The new constitution, the "fundamental law" of the land, was published in December 1819. It established a new state that combined Venezuela and Colombia in one large union under the title of the Republic of Gran Colombia.

During the fall of 1819, at the very moment when the patriots were consolidating their gains after the momentous victory at Boyacá, important events were taking place in Spain. Ferdinand was establishing an autocratic rule against which the liberals were unable to develop any effective resistance. The insurrections in the New World required more attention than the king had been able to give hitherto. But now, toward the close of 1819, Ferdinand was assembling crack troops at the port of Cádiz. On New Year's Day 1820 the Riego revolt (see page 103) dramatically put an end to Ferdinand's hopes of sending an army to suppress the American revolutions.

The news, most welcome to the republicans, was extremely disheartening to Morillo, who was ordered to negotiate with them. The talks dragged on for months, with Bolívar demanding more as those royalist armies still in the field were being defeated or held to a standstill. With no support from home and with desertions to the patriot cause taking place continually, General Morillo capitulated in November 1820; he signed an armistice in the name of Spain. The Liberator could claim a most important diplomatic victory, for the sovereignty of the new republic had been recognized. The moral victory brought temporary, but desperately needed, respite for soldiers and civilians.

Negotiations for a permanent peace broke down despite General Morillo's sincere urging, upon his return to Spain, that continued fighting had little likelihood of success. The reactionary Ferdinand was obdurate, refusing even to meet with Bolívar's emissaries. Meanwhile Bolívar made good use of the time, recruiting and training more men, so that when hostilities were resumed the patriots were thoroughly prepared.

A major battle, one of the more decisive battles for the liberation of Venezuela, took place on the plains of Carabobo, scene of an earlier defeat of Bolívar. Now, in June 1821, Bolívar had massed a trained force of six thousand men, including the veteran foreign legionaries and the superlative llanero cavalrymen. General La Torre was the commander of five thousand royalists occupying the plain; his artillery dominated the valley which Bolívar would have to take in order to reach the plain. The llanero cavalry, accompanied by the British legion, was dispatched to the hills west of the plain, planning to take the Spaniards by surprise from the rear. Under a broiling sun, Páez and his llaneros executed a forced march of two and a half hours up and down steep hills, in the bed of a shallow, swiftly running stream, through tropical shrubs, finally emerging to a position on a hill overlooking the Spaniards in the plain two miles distant. The llanero cavalry charged impetuously but found themselves trapped in a ravine 150 feet below the level of the plain. The Spaniards trained their guns on the ravine and threw in battalions of infantry. The British saved the day, at a frightful cost of lives, by forming their famous hollow square and drawing the enemy's fire upon themselves while Páez's men were able to regroup. The cavalry made its perilous way back up the hill in order to attack the royalists from a more advantageous position. The British held firm, Bolívar attacked frontally, and when the llaneros, with their fearful twelve-foot lances, caught the royalists from the rear, they were unable to withstand the combined onslaught. La Torre could not maintain control, and the disciplined royalist order turned into a rout. The Spaniards were annihilated; many were killed, more deserted and were taken prisoner; only one regiment escaped.

The Battle of Carabobo was the last major engagement of the war in Venezuela. Bolívar marched into Caracas and Valencia fell soon thereafter. By November 1821 all the Spanish forces in Venezuela had capitulated. The terms of surrender permitted the peaceful departure to Spain of those who so desired; the others joined the patriots.

Of all the territory of the old viceroyalty only Quito (Ecuador) remained in Spanish hands. Gran Colombia was free but, Bolívar reasoned, would remain so only if the Spanish forces in the south—in Quito and in Peru—were eliminated.

～

Quito had occupied Bolívar's attention even before the Battle of Carabobo. He had sent an expedition, under the command of Manuel Valdés, to proceed southward through Pasto and thence to Quito, the Ecuadorian capital. But Valdés had been routed in February 1821 and was awaiting reinforcements in southwest Colombia. Bolívar sent additional men and much-needed supplies, led by General Antonio José de Sucre, an experienced Venezuelan of thirty-one. Sucre, a lieutenant in 1812, had fought bravely in a number of campaigns in Venezuela and had been awarded the rank of general. Now, after taking command of the combined forces, Sucre established headquarters at Trapiche. He subsequently proceeded to Guayaquil. That key Ecuadorian port had already been liberated by its inhabitants, who had declared their independence in October 1820.

In March 1822 Bolívar himself, no longer preoccupied with military matters in Gran Colombia, undertook to invade Ecuador, starting out from Popoyán with a mixed force of Venezuelans and Colombians. They traveled through difficult terrain, whose Indian inhabitants—particularly those of the Cauca Valley and in the area of the city of Pasto—were hostile. On April 7 Bolívar defeated royalist forces that had massed at Bombóná. Then he awaited news from General Sucre, who had left Guayaquil to attack Quito.

The ancient Indian city of Quito is located 9,350 feet above sea level, on the slopes of the volcano Pichincha. Nearby are some of the highest mountains in the world: Cotopaxi, 19,247 feet, and Chimborazo, 20,561 feet. The republican armies were to conduct the campaign for Ecuador at extreme altitudes of 9,000 feet and more.

While Bolívar's army harassed the royalists in the north, Sucre approached Quito from the south. At Riobamba, halfway up the Andes, Sucre wrested a brilliant victory from the enemy. Then Sucre's allied army—an international force composed of Venezuelans, Colombians, Ecuadorians, Peruvians, Bolivians, and even some Argentines and Chileans—made their hazardous way along the snowy slopes of giant Cotopaxi in order to descend upon the Spaniards entrenched at the foot of and on the lower slopes of Pichincha. In the morning of May 24, at 14,000 feet above sea level, within sight of Quito, whose inhabitants watched from their rooftops, the Battle of Pichincha was fought, ending in the complete capitulation of the royalists. This was the last major battle for the liberation of the old presidency of Quito.

Quito turned out in full force to greet Bolívar on his triumphant entry on June 18. The multitudes thronged the streets, rockets burst in air, cannon roared, church bells pealed out welcome. The gay scene is imaginatively described by historian Carleton Beals:

All Quito was out, lining the streets, crowding the plazas. The towers were black with spectators. . . . Every balcony was decorated with bunting, rugs, and brocades and filled with families, from grandparents to tiny children. Pinned among the hordes of sandaled Indians in gray and brown and red ponchos, here and there was a grandee, like some lost glittering emperor, in silver embroidered waistcoat, silver buckle breeches, and tricornered hat. Girls in Regency dresses or still newer French styles—waistlines high under their breasts, low, square necklines edged with velvet ribbon or handmade lace—fluttered along the high cathedral terrace fronting the plaza. Near them, shepherded by whitecowled nuns, swarmed pigtailed Indian girls, dressed as angels with silver-tinseled wings, and carrying batons tipped with gold-tinsel stars. . . . The Liberator passed under numerous arches of triumph.*

⌒

It was at about this time that San Martín was experiencing difficulties, both political and military, in Peru; he was looking for help from Bolívar, and left Lima to meet with him at Guayaquil, July 26.

The interview between the two liberators is surrounded by mystery. No one else was present at the talks. The dramatic encounter has been the subject of much scholarly speculation based on subsequent writings of both leaders. What is certain is the outcome of the discussions, which centered around four main issues: whether Peru or Gran Colombia was the legitimate claimant to Guayaquil; the amount of military aid that Gran Colombia would supply to the Peruvian patriots; who would assume the mantle of leadership of the independence movement in Peru—would the two great leaders collaborate, or would one be subordinate to the other?—and San Martín's proposal of a monar-

* Carleton Beals, *Eagles of the Andes* (Philadelphia, 1963), pp. 223–24.

chical form of government in opposition to Bolívar's concept of a republic for Peru.

Since Guayaquil was occupied by Bolívar's forces, the
Argentinian, more soldier than statesman, was not disposed
to argue the legal merits of the case. An accord was reached
by which the port would go to the northern republic.

The amount of military support to come from Colombia
seems to have been determined as part of the decision
reached on the other two issues, a decision affected by
what transpired in Peru during the two days that San
Martín was in Guayaquil. Disturbing news came in a
letter sent to Bolívar by the Colombian delegation in Lima,
and he was quick to show it to San Martín. Monteagudo,
San Martín's lieutenant, had been seized in a coup d'état
executed under the leadership of a discontented patriot,
Riva Agüero. The Peruvian congress had set up a junta to
rule Peru. With Monteagudo out of the picture, a rival
faction in control in Lima, and with Bolívar holding the
military trump card, San Martín felt that his position was
hopeless. Upon reading the contents of the letter he exclaimed, "If this is so, my public life is over . . ."

San Martín promptly departed from Guayaquil and
returned to Lima where, one month later, he resigned his
command and all his titles and retired into private life. He
left for Chile, went on to Buenos Aires, then sailed to a
voluntary exile in Europe. The fate of Peru, perhaps of
the whole continent, was suddenly left in Bolívar's hands.

ᕲᕲᕲ

Of the three viceroyalties in South America, Peru had
been strongly royalist almost to the very end of the wars

for independence. Not until San Martín with a force of non-Peruvians had entered Lima in 1821 had a significant movement towards independence developed. Although Lima and some of the coastal area had been occupied by the patriots, most of Peru and Upper Peru were still under royalist control as late as 1823. Without additional military aid the Peruvian patriots could not drive out the royalist armies.

Bolívar had consented to provide aid, but he could not legally do so until he had received permission from the government of Gran Colombia. He had already acted without permission when he sent Colonel Paz Castillo with a small force to Lima, but, following Bolívar's order, Paz Castillo avoided involving Colombian troops in any Peruvian operations.

Bolívar pressed the Colombian government to approve the sending of military aid to Peru, but he met with considerable resistance. That government was not quick to render support to its southern neighbors because it had its own difficulties. There were still antipatriot garrisons holding out in isolated spots, notably in Maracaibo. In Venezuela there was growing discord between the military and civil arms of government; Páez was heading toward what eventually became a separatist movement. Santander, vice-president of the Gran Colombian union, was troubled with an endless series of political intrigues in Colombia proper. It was not the time to divert troops and money from domestic requirements.

Added to these problems were others no less serious. In the Pasto region the insurrectionists had not been completely subdued. Throughout the year 1823 the Indian leader Agualongo and other guerrilla chieftains led the inhabitants in almost continuous defiance of Colombian authority. In Ecuador people were growing increasingly resentful against the liberators from Colombia who were drafting men into the army and heavily taxing them for the planned expedition into Peru. Ecuadorians wanted to know who would liberate them from the liberators. And in Peru itself violent disagreement broke out between Riva Agüero, who had proclaimed himself president, and the congress, which challenged Agüero's authority. In effect, two governments were in operation, thus further complicating resistance to the powerful Spanish forces in the country.

Fortunately for the patriots, the royalists could not get much aid from Spain at this time. Although Ferdinand, in 1823, had regained absolutist powers, he lacked the resources to strengthen effectively Spanish garrisons in South America. Any hope he had of support from friendly European powers was scotched by the skillful diplomacy of the British, whose powerful fleet was an additional deterrent, and by the promulgation in 1823 of the Monroe Doctrine. Ferdinand had to rely on his limited resources. What little aid he could muster went mainly to reinforce the royalists in Peru.

By the beginning of 1824 the Spanish forces in Peru numbered fourteen to eighteen thousand, divided into three main armies, with General Canterac as commander-in-chief. Bolívar had overcome the many political and financial obstacles in his path and finally was able to amass a mixed army of about eight thousand men, of whom about six thousand were Colombians. He had sent Sucre to Lima, and followed him in September 1823. The major political divisions that plagued Peru were resolved; Riva Agüero and his colleagues were arrested and Bolívar was given full powers by the Peruvian congress. During the next eleven months, other than several minor engagements, military matters were limited to recruiting and training men. Bolívar's principal aim was to prepare to engage the enemy in one full-scale battle that, hopefully, would end the wars for independence.

By the end of July 1824 the bulk of the patriot army was concentrated at Cerro de Pasco, 110 miles north of Lima. From there Bolívar invaded the Valley of Jauja, to the east of Lima, occupied by General Canterac. Canterac was surprised by the patriot army marching towards Jauja along a route that threatened to cut him off from his base. On August 6, a portion of his force was caught in an unfavorable position on the Plain of Junín, northeast of Lima. A great cavalry battle on the plain surrounded by the high mountains ended in the flight of the Spaniards. The serious loss of a considerable part of his cavalry induced Canterac to retreat. He moved towards the ancient city of Cuzco, slowly pursued by the patriots.

Bolívar was now just forty years old. But he felt old; he was ill and terribly fatigued from the hardships of more than a decade of the most arduous military campaigning; and he was preoccupied with political difficulties in Peru and in Colombia. Therefore he appointed General Sucre commander of all Peruvian forces, while he retained dictatorial powers over matters both political and military.

Sucre was general in the field, but required to follow strictly his leader's orders. Specifically he was commanded to keep the army intact; under no conditions was he permitted to split it into smaller units to take advantage of meeting the enemy in minor engagements. Bolívar was still firm in his conviction that the best strategy was to engage the bulk of the royalist army in a major confrontation.

The very capable Sucre felt frustrated by the limitation on his command, especially when several opportunities that he dared not pursue presented themselves in the next weeks. During September, October, and November Sucre engaged in a series of marching maneuvers paralleling those of Canterac, without either committing their armies to combat. Viceroy La Serna amassed a major portion of the royalists near Cuzco, preparing for the showdown, which finally materialized in December.

Although the royalists outnumbered the patriots eight thousand to six thousand, Sucre was eager to accept the challenge dramatically offered on the plains of Ayacucho, halfway between Lima and Cuzco. The details of the famous battle are recounted by one of the participants, General William Miller, in his *Memoirs,* extracts of which follow:

Quinua, an Indian village, is on the western extremity of the plain of Ayacucho, the shape of which is nearly square, about a league in circumference, and flanked right and left by deep, rugged ravines. In the rear of the plain, or towards the west, is a gradual descent of two leagues to the main road. . . . The eastern boundary of the plain is formed by the abrupt and rugged ridge of Condorkanki; which gigantic bulwark, running north and south, overlooks the field of Ayacucho. A little below the summit of this ridge was perched the royalist army.

The liberating army was drawn up on the plain, in front of the Spaniards, at an interval of about a mile, having Quinua in the rear, each corps being formed in close column, to await the attack of the royalists. . . .

During the night of the 8th, a brisk fire was maintained between the royalist and patriot outposts. It was the object of Sucre to prevent the royalists descending in the night. For this purpose the bands of two battalions were sent to the foot of the ridge and continued playing for some time whilst a sharp fire was kept up. This feint had the desired effect, for the royalists did not stir from their lines. . . .

The night of the 8th was one of deep and anxious interest. A battle was inevitable on the following day, and that battle was to decide the destinies of South America. The patriots were aware that they had to contend with twice their own numbers; and that nothing but a decisive victory could save them and their country from ignominious servitude. . . .

The morning of the 9th dawned particularly fine. At first there was a chilliness in the air . . . but when the sun rose above the mountain, the effects of its genial warmth became manifest in the renovated spirits of the soldiers. . . . At nine A.M. the division of Villalobos began to descend. The viceroy, on foot, placed himself at its head; and the files wound down the craggy side of Condorkanki, obliquing a little to their left. The division Monet, forming the royalist right, commenced at the same time to defile directly into the plain. The cavalry, leading their horses, made the same movement, though with greater difficulty, between the infantry of each division. As the files arrived on the plain, they formed into column. . . .

It was during this operation, which had an imposing effect, that Sucre rode along his own line, and, addressing a few emphatic words to each corps, recalled to memory its former achievements. He then placed himself in a central point, and, in an inspiring tone of voice, said, "that upon the efforts of that day depended the fate of South America"; then pointing to the descending columns, he assured his men, "that another day of glory was about to crown their admirable constancy." This animating address of the general produced an electric effect, and was answered by enthusiastic "vivas."

. . . Sucre ordered the division Córdova and two regiments of cavalry to advance to the charge. The gallant Córdova placed himself about fifteen yards in front of his division, formed into four parallel columns with the cavalry in the intervals. Having dismounted, he plunged his sword into the heart of his charger, and turning to the troops, exclaimed, "there lies my last horse; I have now no means of escape, and we must fight it out together!" Then waving his hat above his head, he continued, *"Adelante, con paso de vencedores"* [Forward, with the step of conquerors]. . . . The columns . . . moved to the attack in the finest possible order. The Spaniards stood firmly and full of apparent confidence. The viceroy was seen, as were also Monet and Villalobos, at the head of their division, superintending the formation of their columns as they reached the plain. The hostile bayonets crossed, and for three or four minutes the two parties struggled together, so as to leave it doubtful which would give way. At this moment the Colombian cavalry, headed by Colonel Silva, charged. This brave officer fell covered with wounds, but the intrepidity of the onset was irresistible. The royalists lost ground, and were driven back with great slaughter. The vice-king was wounded and taken prisoner. As the patriots, who had deployed, kept up a well-directed fire, and numbers of the enemy were seen to drop and roll down, till their progress was arrested by the brush-wood, or some jutting crag. . . .

At dawn of day, the royalist division Vadés commenced a detour of nearly a league. Descending the sides of Condorkanki on the north, Valdés had placed himself on the left of the patriots at musket-shot distance, separated by a ravine. At the important moment of the battle, just described, he opened a heavy fire from four field-pieces and a battalion in extended files. By this, he obliged two battalions of the Peruvian division La Mar to fall back. The Colombian battalion Bargas, sent to support the Peruvian division, also began to give way. Two royalist battalions crossed the deep ravine, already spoken of, on the left, and advanced in double quick time in pursuit of the retiring patriots. At this critical juncture, Miller [the author] took upon himself to lead the hussars of Junín against the victorious Spaniards, and by a timely charge drove them back, and followed them across the ravine, by which time he was supported by the *granaderos a caballo* [horse grenadiers] and by the division La Mar, which had rallied. The brave Colonel Plaza crossed the ravine at the head of the legion on the left. Lieutenant-Colonel Moran, at the head of the battalion Bargas, made a similar movement on the right of the cavalry. These two battalions and the cavalry, mutually supporting and rivalling each other in valor, repeated their charges with such resolution, that the division Valdés was broken; its artillery taken; its cavalry obliged to fly in disorder; and its infantry dispersed.

The royalists had now lost the battle, and fled to the ridge from which they had descended, in the morning, with so much confidence.

The action lasted an hour. Fourteen hundred royalists were killed, and seven hundred wounded, and they lost fifteen pieces of artillery.

The loss on the part of the patriots was three hundred and seventy killed, and six hundred and nine wounded. . . .*

* John Miller, *Memoirs of General [William] Miller* (London, 1828), II, pp. 195–204.

The Battle of Ayacucho was the last major battle of the wars for independence. It marked the end of any effective resistance, although small royalist detachments continued to fight for some time in 1825. In Upper Peru, the royalist general Pedro Antonio de Olañeta was easily defeated by General Sucre at the Battle of Tumusla on April 2, 1825. On August 6 an assembly of Upper Peru met and voted in favor of independence from Argentina, which had claimed the province, and from Peru, which had vague aspirations of incorporating it. In honor of the Great Liberator, the assembly named the new nation Bolivia.

The whole of the South American and North American continents were now emancipated from Spanish domination. The Spanish American people were now responsible for their own destinies.

ᴄ～๑

The union that was Gran Colombia had a brief existence. Too many centrifugal forces existed to permit unity. Differences in physical geography, the evolution of nationalism, and the rise of local caudillos were major factors leading to the disintegration of Gran Colombia into three republics.

During Bolívar's absence in Peru and Bolivia, Santander in Colombia and Páez in Venezuela were plotting separation. Bolívar did not return to Bogotá until November 1826, after an absence of five years. He had hardly time to deal with the developing confusion there when he had to hasten to Caracas to deal with the scheming Páez. The Great Liberator accepted at face value Páez's affirmation of loyalty, then returned to Bogotá at the end of 1827. In June 1828, the congress named Bolívar as dictator. But illness and the fatigue born of so many hardships made it even more difficult to deal with continual plots and internal discord. An attempt upon his life almost succeeded. His personal life was the subject of endless scandal. He became thoroughly disillusioned and disheartened. He lamented: "America is ungovernable. Those who have served the revolution have plowed the sea."

Dying of tuberculosis, embittered because of his political failures, Bolívar resolved to leave the country in May 1830. The announcement that he was to exile himself precipitated the dissolution of the union. First Venezuela seceded. Then a cabildo abierto in Quito declared for the independence of Ecuador. Bolívar's grand scheme had come to an end.

Before he could sail to Europe, death overtook Simón Bolívar in Santa Marta on December 17, 1830.

CHAPTER EIGHT

Conclusion

THE EMANCIPATION OF THE SPANISH COLO-
nies did not result in the emancipation of the people.
Political and social democracy did not exist. Dictatorships
flourished in all the new nations during the immediate
postindependence period.

Of all the revolutions, only the Mexican, initially, took
the form of a popular uprising. Its first leaders, Hidalgo
and Morelos, were humanitarians who not only professed
but acted upon ideals of social equality; the battle for those
ideals terminated with their deaths.

With few exceptions the Creole—and even the mestizo—
liberators ignored the needs of the masses of people, or
used them as pawns, or at best mouthed pious declarations
of justice and liberty for all. Such declarations were discarded after the achievement of independence and were
substituted with empty promises of a glorious future.

In many of the republics, Negroes were freed from slavery, an instance of social progress that preceded by decades the parallel achievement in the United States. Behind such emancipation there was often an ulterior motive. Abolition did not always spring from humanitarian impulses or from genuine desires for social reform. Winning the Negroes to fight on one side or another was the practical consideration. San Martín saw the military value of free Negroes fighting for Creole independence. At the battles of Maipú and Chacabuco, for example, almost one-third of the rebel armies were blacks. Bolívar did not see the value of free Negroes until his eyes were opened by the Haitian president. Some Negroes gained their freedom by volunteering their services to royalist officers. To a slave, freedom meant something relatively simple, practical and concrete—the end of chattel slavery; abstract principles of independence had no immediate significance.

It must be acknowledged, however, that abolition of slavery, while it did not resolve all the social problems of Negroes, stands solidly on its own merits as a progressive accomplishment. Emancipation from chattel slavery is a prerequisite to the complete emancipation of the individual.

The fate of the Indians was tragic. Indians had fought on both sides—indeed, the majority of the fighting forces, royalist and patriot, consisted of Indians and mestizos. Sometimes the inducement was the promise, sometimes the fulfillment, of some palliatives, some redress of grievances. Although certain individual patriots thought of eventual social equality for the Indian, the majority of Creoles fought for selfish political and economic interests; they were antagonistic to any proposals of social democracy. It is quite true that fighting afforded an opportunity for some individuals of color to ascend the social ladder; there are many examples of officers and political leaders who were mestizos or mulattoes. But the mass was condemned to hard work and hunger just as they had been before independence.

The continued exploitation of the mass of people, proceeding along lines not fundamentally different from colonial practice, was and is a principal economic reason for the absence of political and social democracy. The aristocracy of the colonies continued to dominate the economic and political life of the independent nations.

The large landed estates, or latifundia, of the privileged class account for the agricultural backwardness of the republics. This system, economically inefficient and socially backward, may be compared with the former slave economy of the southern states of the United States of America. In the north and west of that country, small and medium-sized farms were the rule; in the south, slave plantations were key. In the north and west, agriculture and farmers prospered, the foundation for the prosperity of the larger economy; in the slave south, the economy stagnated. In Spanish America there are a few thousand hacendados and tens of millions of agricultural workers without land. The problems relating to the equitable distribution and efficient use of the land—the agrarian problem with its concomitant social and political problems—constitute the fundamental economic issues in Latin America today.

There are other reasons for the rise of dictatorships in the former colonies. Unlike the Anglo-American colonies, for example, there had been no tradition of democratic process. The democracy of the United States evolved over a long period in political thought and practice. Some liberators, like Bolívar and San Martín, professed beliefs in democratic republics, but argued that the circumstances in Spanish America were not then ripe for the immediate establishment of a full-fledged democratic state. It was true that in South America, governments with strong executives had to be organized during the very course of the struggles for independence. Dictatorship, at least a strong executive, during the wars is understandable; it may even have been necessary. But in Spanish America the absence of democracy before the wars combined with the dictatorships established during the prolonged fighting constituted the historical and practical basis for their continuation in the post-independence period.

Although many lower-ranking clergymen fought in the patriot armies, the hierarchy of the Church had been pro-royalist all during the revolutionary wars. Nevertheless the leaders of the new independent republics did not interfere with Church organization or with the great economic power it continued to enjoy. Catholicism retained its status as the official religion and the only one to be tolerated. So mild a reform as O'Higgins' proposal to permit Protestants to have their own cemeteries was vehemently resisted. Separation of Church and State, one of the hallmarks of modern democracies, was not given any consideration by the new dictators. For the close partnership that had existed between the Spanish monarchy and the Church, there was substituted the intimate relationship between the new Spanish American rulers and the Church. The new despots had no basic conflict with a Church which, while it denied the right to revolution, had endorsed autocracy and even absolute dictatorships.

Still another factor in the evolution of the dictatorships was the rise of caudillos, local political-military chiefs with a great personal following. With the wars being fought over immense expanses of territory, involving different populations with varied economic interests, it was natural that regional military leaders, like Páez and Francia, would emerge. In part, too, caudillismo was a logical continuation of colonial practice; local chieftains who were weeks, even months distant from the centers of colonial power assumed positions of great authority in their own regions. Caudillismo, persisting throughout most of Latin America to this day, is the product of three centuries of Spanish colonial institutions and the military means employed to end Spanish rule. Spanish domination ended, but certain political practices persisted. Dictatorship is a logical outgrowth of caudillismo.

It was not the spirit of liberty that had motivated most Creoles. They had not sought a social revolution. The Spaniards of America had simply replaced the Spaniards of Spain as the new masters.

To say that there was no social revolution, no profound social upheaval, does not mean that there were no major social changes. Slavery was abolished during the wars of independence in some of the colonies and not long after in all the new nations. The aspirations of the upper-class

Creoles were realized and their lower ranks gained some minor advantages. The way was opened for a few mestizos to climb higher on the social ladder. A basis was laid for the potential development of social democracy in that each nation was independent. A nation free from formal imperial overlordship is a necessary precondition for democratic evolution.

For the anticolonial movements of the twentieth century, the American and French revolutions (and, sometimes, the Russian) have been models rather than those of Spanish America. The political-social content of the American Revolution makes it more appealing to the revolutionary colonials of today. The ideals of liberty, equality, and justice and the ideal of representative government expressed in the American Declaration of Independence of 1776 and their more lucid and comprehensive expression in the French *Declaration of the Rights of Man* of 1789 have more significance than the pale borrowings expressed in the Spanish American declarations. It appears perfectly logical for twentieth-century colonial revolutionists to turn to the earlier documents for their inspiration.

Hence the lasting influence of the Spanish American revolutions of independence has not been because of the inspirational effects of expressed ideals. But they have provided colonials with additional major examples to throw off the yoke of colonial servitude. The inspiration they afford is in their very accomplishment.

Should the colonial emancipations be viewed as inconsequential events insofar as the history of freedom is concerned? Must one come to the pessimistic, skeptical conclusion that the emancipation of nations is vain and futile if their peoples are not free?

It is doubtful that the people of a nation can be free if the entire nation is enslaved. The emancipation of nations is the historical prelude for the emancipation of peoples.

At the close of the seventh decade of the twentieth century, the stirrings towards freedom of colonies and subjects nations is still part of the historical evolution that began in the eighteenth century. The American, French, and Spanish American revolutions transformed a world still undergoing revolutionary change. In those instances where independence has come recently to the countries of Asia and Africa, the emancipation of their peoples is still to be put on the agenda of history. The independence of all the *nations* of the world is still to be achieved, but this goal is in sight. The emancipation of the *peoples* of the world, however, seems a long, long way off.

Glossary

Bibliography

Chronology

Index

✐ GLOSSARY

alcabala: sales tax
audiencia: high administrative and judicial court
cabildo: municipal council
cabildo abierto: open meeting of municipal council
cacique: Indian chieftain
caudillo: military or political leader
caudillismo: government system dependent on the caudillo
chapetón: derogatory term applied to European-born Span-
    iards residing in the colonies
comuneros: commoners
cordillera: mountain range
corregidor: colonial governor of a municipal district and its
    immediate environs
cortes: Spanish parliament
criollo: Creole, white born in the New World
estancia: cattle ranch in Argentina, Uruguay
fundo: rural estate, Chile
gachupín: derogatory term applied to European-born Span-
    iards residing in the colonies

gaucho: plains cowboy, originally a nomad, in Argentina, Uruguay

grito: outcry, cry of protest

hacendado: owner of a hacienda

hacienda: landed estate

huaso: Chilean cowboy

inquilino: tenant farmer, Chile

junta: a committee

latifundiium: large landed property

llanero: plainsman, Venezuela

maté: Paraguayan tea

mestizo: offspring of white and Indian

mulato: offspring of white and Negro

obraje: textile factory

peninsular: New World resident born in the Spanish peninsula

peón: day laborer

porteño: resident in the port of Buenos Aires

rancho: farm, ranch

repartimiento: mandatory purchase of merchandise by Indians from colonial officials

roto: (broken, ragged) Chilean peón

tumulto: tumult, riot

vaquero: cowboy, herdsman

visitador: Spanish official authorized to inspect or investigate a viceroyalty or captaincy-general

zambo: offspring of Indian and Negro

↶ BIBLIOGRAPHY
OF BOOKS IN ENGLISH

ARCINIEGAS, GERMAN. *Latin America, A Cultural History* (New York, Knopf, 1966).

BANCROFT, HUBERT H. *History of Mexico* (San Francisco, 1883–88). 6 vols.

BEALS, CARLETON. *Eagles of the Andes* (Philadelphia, Chilton, 1963).

BELAÚNDE, V. A. *Bolívar and the Political Thought of the Spanish American Revolution* (Baltimore, Johns Hopkins, 1938).

BERNSTEIN, HARRY. *Modern and Contemporary Latin America* (Philadelphia, Lippincott, 1945).

CARUSO, JOHN A. *The Liberators of Mexico* (New York, Pageant Press, 1954).

COCHRANE, THOMAS. *Memoranda of Naval Services in the Liberation of Chile and Peru from Spanish Domination* (London, 1858).

DIFFIE, BAILEY W. *Latin American Civilization* (Harrisburg, Pa., Stackpole, 1945).

EDWARDS, AGUSTÍN. *The Dawn* (London, Benn, 1931).

FISHER, LILLIAN E. *The Background of the Revolution for Mexican Independence* (Boston, Christopher, 1934).

GALDAMES, LUIS. *A History of Chile,* trans. and ed. by I. J. Cox (Chapel Hill, University of North Carolina Press, 1941).

GIBSON, CHARLES. *Spain in America* (New York, Harper, 1966).

GRAHAM, R. B. CUNNINGHAME. *José Antonio Páez* (London, Heinemann, 1929).

HAMILL, HUGH M., JR. *The Hidalgo Revolt* (Gainesville, University of Florida, 1966).

HARING, CHARLES H. *The Spanish Empire in America* (New York, Oxford, 1947).

HASBROUCK, ALFRED. *Foreign Legionaries in the Liberation of Spanish South America* (New York, Columbia University, 1928).

HENAO, J. M., and ARRUBLA, G., *History of Colombia,* trans. and ed. by J. F. Rippy (Chapel Hill, University of North Carolina, 1938).

HERRING, HUBERT. *A History of Latin America,* 3d ed. (New York, Knopf, 1968).

HUMBOLDT, ALEXANDER VON. *A Political Essay on the Kingdom of New Spain,* trans. and ed. by John Black (London, 1811). 4 vols.

———. *Personal Narrative of Travels to the Equinoctial Regions of the New Continent,* trans. by Helen M. Williams (London, 1814–29). 7 vols.

HUMPHREYS, R. A., and LYNCH, JOHN, eds. *The Origins of the Latin American Revolutions* (New York, Knopf, 1966).

JOHNSON, JOHN J. *Simón Bolívar and Spanish American Independence* (Princeton, Van Nostrand, 1968).

JUAN, JORGE, and ULLOA, ANTONIO DE. *A Voyage to South America,* trans. by John Adams (London, 1806). 2 vols.

KEEN, BENJAMIN, ed. *Readings in Latin American Civilization* (Boston, Houghton Mifflin, 1955).

KIRKPATRICK, F. A. *A History of the Argentine Republic* (Cambridge, Cambridge University Press, 1931).

LECUNA, VICENTE, and BIERCK, HAROLD, eds. *Selected Writings of Bolívar* (New York, Colonial Press, 1951).

LEVENE, RICARDO A. *A History of Argentina,* trans. and edited by William S. Robertson (Chapel Hill, University of North Carolina, 1957).

MADARIAGA, SALVADOR DE. *Bolívar* (London, Hollis and Carter, 1952).

———. *The Fall of the Spanish American Empire* (New York, Macmillan, 1947).

MASUR, GERHARD. *Simón Bolívar* (Albuquerque, University of New Mexico Press, 1948).

METFORD, J. C. J. *San Martin the Liberator* (Blackwell, Oxford, 1950).

MILLER, JOHN, ed. *Memoirs of General [William] Miller,* 2 vols. (London, 1828).

MITRE, BARTOLOMÉ. *The Emancipation of South America,* trans. by William Pilling (London, Chapman, 1893).

MOSES, BERNARD. *The Intellectual Background of the Revolutions in South America* (New York, Hispanic Society of America, 1926).

———. *South America on the Eve of Independence* (New York, Putnam, 1908).

———. *Spain's Declining Power in South America* (Berkeley, Calif., University of California Press, 1919).

PARRY, J. H. *The Spanish Seaborne Empire* (New York, Knopf, 1966).

PICÓN-SALAS, MARIANO. *A Cultural History of Spanish America,* trans. by Irving A. Leonard (Berkeley, Calif., University of California, 1963).

ROBERTSON, WILLIAM S. *The Life of Miranda* (Chapel Hill, University of North Carolina: Chapel Hill, 1929). 2 vols.

———. *Iturbide of Mexico* (Durham, N.C., Duke University, 1952).

———. *Rise of the Spanish American Republics* (New York, Collier, 1961).

ROJAS, RICARDO. *San Martín, Knight of the Andes*, trans. by
    H. Brickell and C. Videla (New York, Doubleday, 1945).
SHERWELL, G. A. *Antonio José de Sucre* (Washington, D.C.,
    B. S. Adams, 1924).
SPRAGUE, W. F. *Vicente Guerrero, Mexican Liberator* (Chicago,
    R. R. Donnelly, 1939).
TIMMONS, W. H. *Morelos of Mexico* (El Paso, University of
    Texas West, 1968).
TREND, J. B. *Bolivar and the Independence of Spanish America*
    (New York, Harper, 1968).
WARREN, H. G. *The Sword Was Their Passport* (Baton Rouge,
    Louisiana State University, 1943).
————. *Paraguay* (Norman, University of Oklahoma, 1949).
WHITAKER, ARTHUR P., ed. *Latin America and the Enlighten-
    ment* (Ithaca, N.Y., Cornell University Press, 1961).

✑ CHRONOLOGICAL TABLES

1. BOURBON DYNASTY (Spanish branch)

1700–1746	Philip V
1746–1759	Ferdinand VI
1759–1788	Charles III
1788–1808	Charles IV
1808–1813	[Joseph Bonaparte]
1813–1833	Ferdinand VII

✑

2. WARS INVOLVING SPAIN

1701–15	War of Spanish Succession
1718–20	War against France and England
1727–29	War against France and England
1733–38	War against Austria
1739–41	War of Jenkins' Ear, merges into War of Austrian Succession
1740–48	War of Austrian Succession

1756–63	Seven Years' War
1793–95	War against France
1796–1800	War against England
1799	Aid to American colonies during revolution against England
1801	War against Portugal
1805	War against England
1807–13	Resistance to Napoleonic invasion
1823	France invades Spain

⌒⌒

3. PRINCIPAL EVENTS IN SPAIN AND SPANISH AMERICA

1767	Jesuits expelled from Spanish America
1780	Uprising of Tupac Amarú II; revolt of the comuneros
1794	Antonio Nariño publishes translation of Declaration of Rights of Man
1802	Bernardo O'Higgins returns to Chile
1806	Miranda's expedition to Venezuela
	First English invasion of Buenos Aires
1807	Bolívar returns from Europe to Venezuela
	Second English invasion of Buenos Aires
1808	Charles IV abdicates; Ferdinand VII imprisoned by Napoleon
	May 2: anti-French uprising in Madrid; Central Junta formed to rule Spain in absence of Ferdinand VII
	September: Viceroy Iturrigaray deported from New Spain
1809	September: Mariano Moreno publishes tract advocating free trade
1810	April: Junta established in Caracas (Venezuela); Spanish authority defied
	May 25: *De facto* independence of La Plata
	July: Paraguayans reject Buenos Aires leadership

	July 20: New Granada (Colombia) declares in-dependence
	September 16: Grito de Dolores—Hidalgo initi-ates revolution in Mexico
	September 18: Junta formed in Chile
1811	June: Paraguay declares independence
	July: Venezuela declares independence
	July 30: Hidalgo executed
1812	March: Cortes in Spain proclaims liberal con-stitution
	Fall: Bolívar returns from exile to Cartagena
1813	Spring: Bolívar invades Venezuela from New Granada
	October: Bolívar declared Liberator of Vene-zuela
1814	Ferdinand VII returns to Spanish throne; abol-ishes Constitution of 1812
	July: Bolívar flees to Cartagena
	October: Battle of Rancagua (Chile)
	November 27: Morelos executed
1815	May: Bolívar goes to Jamaica
1816	Spring: Bolívar returns to Venezuela from Haiti
	July 9: Buenos Aires declares independence
1817	January: San Martín and O'Higgins cross Andes into Chile
	February: Battle of Chacabuco (Chile)
1818	February 12: Chile formally declares independ-ence
	April: Battle of Maipú (Chile)
1818–19	Bolívar's westward march across the Andes into New Granada
1819	August: Battle of Boyacá (Venezuela)
1820	January 1: Army revolts in Spain; Constitution of 1812 again proclaimed
	August 20: San Martín and fleet depart from Valparaíso for Peru

1821	February: Plan of Iguala
	June: Second Battle of Carabobo (Venezuela)
	July: San Martín enters Lima; independence of Peru declared
	Gran Colombia formed, union of Colombia and Venezuela
	September 27: Independence of Mexico achieved
1822	March: Bolívar invades Ecuador
	April: Battle of Bomboná (Ecuador)
	May: Battle of Pichincha (Ecuador)
	May 21: Iturbide crowned Agustin I, Emperor of Mexico
	May 29: Ecuador proclaims its incorporation into Gran Colombia
	July: Bolívar and San Martín meet at Guayaquil
1823	Ferdinand VII restores absolute despotism in Spain
	Central American Federation secedes from Mexico
1824	August: Battle of Junín (Peru)
	December: Battle of Ayacucho (Peru)
1825	August: Bolivia declares independence
1826	October: Sucre elected president of Bolivia
1828	Uruguay (Banda Oriental) achieves independence
1830	Venezuela, Colombia, and Ecuador separate
1838	Nicaragua, Costa Rica, and Honduras secede from Central American Federation
1839	Guatemala and El Salvador form separate republics

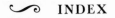 INDEX

DATE DUE